ALL THINGS ARE POSSIBLE WITH CROHN'S

Enjoy Living the Life of Your Dreams

Carroll Regan deCarle

ISBN: 0988270005
ISBN 13: 9780988270008
Library of Congress Control Number: 2012949333
Leading Edge Management Sarasota, FL

DEDICATION TO ART

With much love, admiration and gratitude, I thank you for your many years of sacrifices on my behalf. Without you this book would never have come to fruition. I thank you for understanding my weaknesses, yet loving me in spite of them. I thank you for slogging alongside me through all our fields of battle, forever raising our flag of victory. Never once giving up, nor giving in. When my skies grew dark with uncertainties, you promised the sun would again make a spectacular entrance bringing with it hope and serenity. You, my wonderful husband, my best friend, have never broken your promise. May the sun shine forever on the horizons of all your tomorrows and may God enrich your life with all His blessings.

I love you,

Carroll

TABLE OF CONTENTS

Prologue.. VII

Chapter 1 **THE BEGINNING** – Barrington, Illinois - 1970 3

Chapter 2 5

Chapter 3 7

Chapter 4 11

Chapter 5 17

Chapter 6 21

Chapter 7 27

Chapter 8 31

Chapter 9 37

Chapter 10 41

Chapter 11 43

Chapter 12 49

Chapter 13 53

Chapter 14 55

Chapter 15 59

Chapter 16 63

Chapter 17 69

Chapter 18 71

Chapter 19 73

Chapter 20 77

Chapter 21 **THE MIDDLE** – Sarasota, Florida – 2002 85

Chapter 22 89

Chapter 23 93

Chapter 24 99

Chapter 25 105

Chapter 26 111

Chapter 27 115

Chapter 28 119

Chapter 29 123

Chapter 30 129

Chapter 31 **THE PRESENT 2012**....................................135

Chapter 32 137

Chapter 33 141

Chapter 34 145

Chapter 35 147

Chapter 36 153

Chapter 37 157

Chapter 38 161

Chapter 39 165

Chapter 40 169

Chapter 41 171

Chapter 42 173

Epilogue: To Alexander deCarle West 175

Resources: Crohn's/Colitis, Ileostomies, Colostomies, Urostomies, & Cancer groups in USA, Canada & International, Plus selected books 177

Intimacy for Men and Women
Special Section devoted entirely to adult patients with Ileostomies, Colostomies and Urostomies including Hints for Men and Women Intimate Apparel for Men and Women plus regular apparel for Children and youth..181

Acknowledgements 192

PROLOGUE

I have a story to share with you. But before I can take you forward, I must first take you back. Back more than forty years. I know it was a long time ago and for many of you, well, you probably weren't even born yet. But please stick with me and I promise to reveal the end of the story in due time.

More than forty years ago my life changed . . . and it changed forever.

The summer of 1970 had officially ended and seemed reluctant to yield to autumn patiently waiting in the wings.

We had just arrived home to Barrington, Illinois, from Canada, where we had our summer home. We'd closed it up and made arrangements with friends to use it as often as they wanted during the winter. They were avid snowmobilers and having the luxury of a winterized home to use during the cold north winters for ice skating and snowmobiling, was a treat for them. All they had to do in return was keep the snow off the roof and the oil tank filled with fuel, and the woodpile filled with wood for the fireplace.

Our summers in Canada on the Rideau Lake outside of Smiths Falls, Ontario, near the tiny village of Lombardi, were some of the happiest in my life.

Each summer was different in its own way. Some hotter than others. Some cooler.

But, no matter the weather, when we arrived in early June, our station wagon filled with two kids and a dog, blankets and pillows for sleepy little heads, snacks for everyone including our German Shepherd, Heidi, and our equally filled boat which trailed behind our car, our cottage was always ready for us. Our friends made sure we had fresh linens on the beds, in the bathroom, and an assortment of food to keep us fed until I could go into town to the market and do some serious shopping.

The cottage was situated high on a knoll overlooking the lake. Below was a dock, a long concrete seawall for tying up boats, fishing, or just sunbathing. At the far end of the seawall was our boathouse. A wooden dock and a swim ladder down into the lake allowing for quick access into and out of the crystal clear water. The boathouse was situated with a back-slanted roofline enabling the kids to climb the attached ladder onto the sloping roof which then flattened out allowing them to jump off into the deep water below. Jumping off that boathouse roof was the highlight of everyone's summer. Oh, yeah, the grown-ups enjoyed it just as much as the kids. After all, a grown-up is nothing more than a big kid.

On the far side of the boat house was a small shallow cove for little ones to play. Years of undulating waves relentlessly polished the stones in the children's wading cove. While on the opposite side of the cove, in the lake's crystal clear water, an old weeping willow sat along the shore washing her hair, swaying back and forth as graceful as a ballerina.

Beyond the dense stand of great pines that separated here from there, lay the rest of humanity. But here we existed in our own little world, oblivious to any outside influences, safe in our snug retreat. It was a place where time stood still. Each day filled with laughter, smiles, love, and simply . . . *being*. Alive with the natural beauty that surrounded us while enveloping us in her arms.

Courtney and Mac always had someone to play with. Their cousins summered just down the lane in their large family compound of several cottages and boathouses. Both kids and grown-ups would spend hour upon hour swimming or maybe just floating around on our rubber rafts and huge truck tubes which Uncle Ross and Uncle Jim always seemed to have in great supply. We would water ski and go tubing behind Uncle Ross's jet boat. Why those kids didn't turn into prunes was a mystery. They never wanted to get out of the water. For Courtney and Mac, taking a bar of soap, a bottle of shampoo, a wash cloth, and a towel to the lake was heaven on earth. Once they discovered this new method of bathing it was nearly impossible to get them into the tub or shower.

We would spend most evenings sitting around a campfire, roasting marshmallows, playing horseshoes, and telling stories of Art, Ross, Jim, and their friends and their escapades growing up at the lake each summer. The stories were endless and our sides would ache from laughter. Aunt Doris, the matriarch of the group, had an old piano which she played beautifully. Everyone would gather in her cottage living room, sing songs, dance and tell stories almost every night.

Art was always able to spend five weeks or so of his summer vacation enjoying uninterrupted fun with his family and friends. The rest of his summer was spent commuting from Chicago to Ottawa and on to the cottage. Art had spent his childhood summers on the Rideau. In fact, his family happened to have rented the very cottage that we now owned. Talk about deja vu.

In the fall of 1968, while visiting Ross, his wife, Carol, and baby Leslie, at their cottage, Art and I took a walk down the lane and came upon Art's boyhood cottage. There was a "For Sale" sign in the yard. We took down the phone number, called the realtors, and became proud owners of the lake house.

Another friend of Arts' owned a furniture store. He measured the place; we selected carpeting and furniture all to be installed by next summer. The old couple living in the now winterized cottage year round was able to stay until winter's end. After they moved out, our friend moved in his crew and got the place ready for our summer arrival.

Each summer I would plant boxes of flowers on both sides of the long stone walkway to the dock, along the terraced back wall of the dockside patio, and all the way to the end of the sea wall which was below our screened-in porch.

Beautiful graceful flowers opened wide, radiant . . . alive on steady stems. Little pansies with their sassy little faces, sneered at all who gazed upon them. A cavalcade of geraniums in spectacular bloom lined the terrace overlooking the dock, while pots of petunias were strategically placed everywhere. We'd sit on the lawn or at the dock enjoying the free and limitless expanses opening out into vast distances abound with water and trees.

Our lake house sat on the bank of Miller's Bay. Looking out across the water to the head of the bay lay Miller's farm with its gently rolling fields of crumpled green velvet. Trees stretched tall against the morning sky. Great fields of green led down to the lake. Colorful splashes of flowers dotted the shoreline of the lake front cottages. And, oh, how we loved sitting on the screened porch at night listening to the cry of the loons on the lake while its waters lapped at the rocks below, enjoying the sounds of the wind as it rustled through the trees. The wind told its own ghost stories. We loved the feel of the lazy breeze as it blew in off the water on a hot humid evening.

The days were balmy in the middle and a little crisp around the edges, days when we had to swab the perspiration from little faces as well as our own.

Nights were oftentimes warm with moisture and made sleeping as though in a steam bath. We used our poor fans so often some summers, that they seemed to adopt a disapproving attitude as they shook their heads slowly from side to side as if to remind us that they, too, needed a break. We almost needed gills to survive the humidity.

The summers weren't always a steamy cauldron. We had many cool and refreshing summers. Some were even downright cold at night. But no matter what they were, they were ours and we adapted.

Living in the forest provided an unending supply of strange wild creatures lurking about. Raccoons at night seeing what trouble they could get into, garbage wise. They were such scavengers that we had to keep our trash in a storage room until it was picked up.

Porcupines and skunks were the most worrisome for me. I worried about the kids and the dog. Heidi loved chasing anything with four legs. Even some two-legged, two winged critters as well. It made no difference. If it moved, it was fair game. Each morning she'd peruse her yard checking to see who'd been brave enough during the night to invade her territory, forever vacuuming the lawn with her nose.

Through green coats of whispering meadows we loved listening as the horses whinnied and the cows lowed in the pastures. Our little kitten, Muffin, lay quietly on Courtney's bed licking her paws while gracefully smoothing out her overnight wrinkles.

The kids kept watch as their friendly chubby squirrel busied itself banking its earnings for the winter. A gaggle of geese grouped near the waters edge on the far off shore. Ducks made their usual three-point landing while water-skiing to a stop. Jays called stridently while a couple of gullible crows watched curiously from the farmer's fence. It was always interesting to listen to the shrieking sounds of the birds searching for a place to spend the night safely from the predators of the dark.

There always seemed something magical about the Canadian skies. The sky of day was like a stark unexplored throng of blue, dappled with white cotton candy clouds towing their shadows over the hills. Cotton ball clouds lazily wiped up spilled sunlight while gliding composed and nobly overhead.

At night, when the moon chased away the sun, moonlight changed the dynamic of the landscape to a delicate sculpture while its beams lit the area with a mystical silence. Nighttime was especially magical for the kids. We'd lie on blankets on the lawn, or sit around a roaring fire outside and look up at the sky above enjoying her stellar garden. Thousands upon thousands of stars dusted the huge arc of heaven. You couldn't help but feel close to the heartbeat of the universe as you lay there in the grass looking helplessly into the glittering sky. If you were lucky enough you might even witness a shooting star scratching its fire across the sky, while a trillion diamonds gleamed as they've done for thousands of years. Most evenings, Courtney and Mac would close their eyes tightly, hold hands and wish upon the night's first star.

If you listened carefully, a far away owl may fill the night with questions as it sat safely somewhere on a tree's branch waiting and listening to the eerie sounds of darkness while turning its head like some mechanical stuffed toy, back and forth . . . back and forth.

The dark was also filled with fear as the bats darted through the air, especially around the inside of our boathouse. The kid's refused to go anywhere near it after sundown. They weren't the only ones. Those damn bats scared the heck out of me, too, as they swooped, flapped, dodged, and darted all over the place. But, they weren't the only scary things. Every evening when the sun went down and the bats came out, confused giant moths performed their nocturnal ceremony and kamikazed our porch lights with reckless abandon while terrorizing anyone brave enough to venture inside.

But the most fun for the kids were the fireflies dancing with their light bulbs loose. They looked like they were sewing sequins in the dark. Squeals of laughter filled the darkness as kids ran all over the lawn with their lidded jars to catch their lightning bugs.

What a great experience for the children to get up close and personal with nature. No television to waste their summer watching. Oh, they weren't pleased about that. But before long, they realized that there was life without television. Their days were filled with swimming, playing and just having fun. Their nights were filled with bonfires, quiet rides in the boat, roasting marshmallow and hot dogs, and the ever present catching of fireflies. Rainy days were spent either inside or on the porch reading or playing with their cousins. Those ten summers spent there were amazing. Life for everyone was truly delicious.

As delicious as it was, mundane chores like going into town to do marketing or banking, still had to be done, and there was only one way to get there.

Above our cottage, the little dirt lane skipped off along its merry way, disappearing beyond the endless forest, to the paved road hidden high above our little lane. The road took us from the idyllic life of the lake, our safe otherworld, to the noise of Smiths Falls, bringing us quickly back to reality. Needless-to-say, our trips to town were quick. It was always difficult to leave the serenity of our peaceful cottage life where the scenery remained unedited by the seasons.

Yes, I remember those times vividly like they're photographs I looked at often. Life couldn't have been any better. At least that's what I thought as we sadly said farewell to the summer of 1970, locked the cottage, got back on the road, and headed home to Barrington, Illinois.

THE BEGINNING Barrington, Illinois - 1970

Chapter 1

School would begin in less than a week and Courtney was entering Kindergarten. She was four years old, not to be five, until February. I could scarcely believe my baby was going to school.

Mac, was nine months old and was thinking about walking; thinking, being the operative word, as he was in no hurry to do anything but crawl. And could that child move! I've never seen anyone travel on all fours as fast as he did. It had become his favorite method of transportation. We were certain he would *never* learn to walk. Why would he want to? He could go lickety-split all over the place.

Art was an airline pilot with a major airline. This, of course, meant as a former airline stewardess, turned fulltime wife and mom, I was in charge of keeping up with two small children and one very large German Shepherd. While Art was busy keeping the skies friendly, I was busy keeping all things quiet on the home front.

Life was good. Very good. Little did I know that I would soon be faced with a life altering disease. A disease which little, to nothing, was known except that it was *incurable*.

CHAPTER 2

From September on, I began noticing considerable symptoms like abdominal pain in varying strengths. More frequent bouts of diarrhea and nausea and feeling so sick that no matter what I did I could not seem to get better. I kept thinking maybe it would go away. And for short intervals, the symptoms did. But not for long. Surely it was something that I'd eaten or was eating that was giving me such horrible discomfort. What else could it possibly be? I'd prided myself in serving my family well-balanced, healthy meals. No junk food, except for the obligatory infrequent trips to McDonalds as a treat for the kids.

I kept putting off going to the doctor. After all, I was sure he'd confirm what I'd already known . . . it was only indigestion. Right? Not quite.

After much soul-searching and self-diagnosis, at the end of October Art informed me that it was time to stop playing doctor and actually call one.

He said, quite sternly, "Carroll, don't put it off any longer. Make the damn call or I'll make it for you."

I kinda got the picture. Loud and clear. I acquiesced, made the call, and got an appointment in November.

CHAPTER 3

November came roaring in with snow and bitter cold weather. The kind of cold that showed no mercy. Chicago could be brutal in the winter and today was no exception.

The morning I left home for my doctor appointment in Evanston on the north shore of Chicago, snow churned out of the heavens turning the roads into a carpet of white. Swirls of the powdery white stuff kicked up by intermittent gusts made driving a challenge. Dangerous . . . but beautiful. Snow banks glared white while fluffy-filled arms of evergreens bent and swayed with the wind. I always found it rather curious as how something as delicate and beautiful could be so deadly.

Ordinarily the trip should take less than an hour; today it would take me closer to two.

Frozen wind howled through the slanting snow making it difficult to navigate from the parking lot to my doctor's office. It was so bloody cold I was sure my eyeballs would freeze. I felt like I was in my own snow globe. How I wished I were at home sitting in front of a cozy, roaring fire. However, I didn't have that option. My abdominal pains were growing in intensity. Subsiding occasionally but never fully going away. Each time they came back, they'd come back with a vengeance. Oh, I was more than ready to see the doctor. No more excuses. No more self-diagnosis. Something was happening and it wasn't good.

My doctor told me that I probably had what was known as colitis, which is an inflammation of the colon portrayed by lower-bowel spasms and upper-bowel cramps.

But I already knew about colitis. I'd had it for years. I was using Librax to lessen the spasms in my intestine. At times Librax worked just fine, other times, not so much. To be certain, however, he suggested I see a specialist. The appointment was made for me that day, making sure, I guess, that I would actually go and not leave it up to me.

Two days later, I found myself face-to-face with a specialist who happened to be an acquaintance of Art. Now I knew for sure I was in real trouble. There would be no possibility of wiggling out of missing any appointments or of not telling Art the whole story. Arnold would make sure Art knew everything I knew.

After a series of tests, it was confirmed that I did have colitis. I was put on a regimen of medicines and a special diet. No roughage of any kind, no dairy products, nothing fried and nothing spicy.

"What!" I said, stunned. "That pretty much eliminates everything I eat. Good grief, Arnold." I was ready to strangle him as I popped out of my chair and began pacing the office. "And furthermore, I have never been on a diet in my life. Look at me. Do you honestly think I look like I need to go on a diet? I'm five feet nine and carry a very proud weight of one hundred twenty five pounds. And that's after having two children and one of them just a year ago."

The doctor could see the frustration on my face and hear the indignation in my voice. But, being a gentle and very caring man, he allowed my ramblings to go on without interruption.

He waited until I was through before asking, "Are you finished? If not, continue and I'll just sit here and wait. You let me know, okay?"

Embarrassed, I timidly responded, "Yes, Arnold, I'm finished." I slowly slithered into my chair.

"Okay. Now let's start over. Your diet has nothing to do with your weight. It has, however, everything to do with your health. And that is my only concern. It should be yours as well. Are we on the same page now?" he asked with a gentle smile.

"We're on the same page. Sorry for getting off script there." I answered, simply mortified.

"Good! Now let me go over this diet with you and I'll be happy to answer any and all questions. Then we'll go over your medications."

I listened and asked questions. Lots of questions. He very patiently and thoroughly explained everything until he was confident I would follow his instructions.

"I'm starting you off slowly with a couple of drugs to see if we can get this thing under control. One is prednisone, which is a steroid to help reduce inflammation. The other is a sulfa drug, sulfasalazine which reduces the chance of a flare-up. Between the two, we should get a fairly good handle on this." He handed me the two prescriptions.

"The next script is Librax. It will calm your spastic gut making you more comfortable."

"This one is for Lomotil. It's to control your diarrhea. Don't hesitate to take it. From what you tell me, you have been experiencing far too many bouts of diarrhea and we need to get that under control." He handed me the next one.

"Okay, this is your last one. It's Phenergan and it's for nausea. I know this seems like a whole lot to take in, but please follow all the instructions, okay? And, Carroll, call if you notice any changes in your bowels or your gut other than what you're already experiencing. Alright?"

"Alright," I said, fighting to keep my voice steady. "I think I have it all and I can assure you that this conversation will definitely not be coming up at the next cocktail party." Everything was swirling around inside my head like a whirlwind.

"Good girl. Please give my best to Art and have him give me a call. Here's my home phone number, even though he already has it. But in case he's misplaced it, you'll have it for him."

"Thanks Arnold, for seeing me so quickly. I really appreciate it."

"Anytime, Carroll," he said standing, coming around his desk, and escorting me to the appointment desk. "The girls will make your next appointment for you. I want you to have a blood panel done and if everything looks okay, I'll see you again in two weeks, alright?"

"Sure." I took the order for the blood tests which had to be done before my next appointment.

I was about to leave when the doctor came back out. "I want you to call if you have any concerns or if you notice any changes at all. So please pay attention to those things, okay? It's really important that you do so."

"I promise." I said. "And, Arnold, thanks for putting up with my diatribe."

"Put it out of your mind. I already have," he said with a smile.

We said our goodbyes. I was off, already feeling better and pleased that I went. It wasn't as bad as I thought it would be, after all.

Alone in the elevator, I leaned against the back wall shaking my head. "God, Carroll, what a dip you were, going on and on about a damn diet. He must think Art really married a ding-a-ling." I laughed at myself. How could I not?

CHAPTER 4

In the days that followed, I found myself feeling a little better. The diet was working. But, like any diet, it was a drudge. Not only could I not have salads, and most vegetables, but no dairy which meant no ice cream cones. Bummer! Also no spicy foods like pasta, pizza, or the kids' favorites, tacos. And, absolutely, positively, no popcorn. I sure loved my popcorn. But no more.

Heck, I couldn't even have a cocktail. Oh, what fun I was going to have at the next party. Not that I was a big drinker, mind you. I wasn't. But now and again, I loved a cocktail or a glass of wine or champagne. Not all at the same time, of course, that would definitely have been a sight for sore eyes. Nope, just a one-of-a-kind kinda gal. Well, maybe two-of-a-kind kinda gal. I was becoming what you might call a serial sipper. At parties, no one knew that I was drinking only seven-up or ginger ale. They couldn't tell if it was my first drink or my tenth.

Yes indeedy, I had definitely cornered the market on that serial sipping thing.

My two week appointment arrived. I again found myself back in Evanston and sitting in the doctor's office. Arnold sat at his desk going over my blood work results, drumming his manicured nails on my opened chart.

"Well, how am I doing so far?" I asked.

"Not too bad," he replied.

"That's good, right?" I asked smiling.

"Like I said, not bad; but what I want to hear now is how have you been doing on the meds and the diet? Let's start with your meds first."

"Alright, I guess. Never having taken them before, I have no point of reference." I answered the best I could.

"Okay, then let me ask some questions. How's your cramping? Are you having more, less, or no change at all?"

"At times I feel pretty good, and other times, it's pretty bad."

"How bad? Worse than before bad or about the same bad?" He asked with a voice full of concern. "And, Carroll, the truth please. Not what you think I *want* to hear, but what I *need* to hear. We've got to work together or you'll never get well. Okay?"

"Okay." I said not really wanting to tell him the truth.

"Let's hear it. All of it. First, tell me about your pain."

"In the beginning, I was feeling so much better. I had less pain and less frequently. I figured the diet and the meds were working. And to a degree, I guess they were. Until a few days ago, that is."

"What changed?" he asked, sitting much straighter in his chair.

"The abdominal pain increased substantially. The pains were becoming more intense. Sharper. Much sharper, and for longer intervals. I was also becoming quite nauseous at those times. One day, I . . . I . . ." I couldn't go any further. Tears began to slowly slide down my cheeks.

In a very quiet and calming voice the doctor asked, "Tell me, Carroll. And, what?"

"I had blood in my stools."

"How much blood?" he asked.

"Not much, just enough that it frightened me. So, I began checking each time I had a bowel movement, which seemed to be more frequently than usual. I'd notice blood on the toilet tissue. Is all this normal?" I asked dabbing my eyes with a tissue I'd removed from the box on his desk.

"If you have hemorrhoids, yes. But what I'm going to do is tweak your meds and I want you to keep a record of how you're feeling, pain wise. More severe. Less severe. That sort of thing.

Also, tell me, are you having diarrhea more or less frequently since our last visit? You've only talked about blood in your stools."

"It seems I'm not having many formed stools anymore. Mostly diarrhea now. I think that's how I was able to see the blood."

"That explains a lot. I cannot emphasize strongly enough, that you must tell me everything. Every little thing, especially the things you don't think are important. Because to me it may be the one thing that holds the key to unlocking what in hell's the problem. That one crucial pivotal point I'm looking for to piece this puzzle together. It's *that* important. I know keeping a journal on a daily basis can be a real pain in the ass, pardon the pun. Just keep in mind, it's your ass! Blunt I know, but true," he said with a grin as he tilted his head.

"Yeah, I get it."

"Good. I hope you also get that when I said to call me, I meant for you to do just that. Call me. Don't wait and play doctor. Until you get your medical degree, I'm still in charge here. Understood?" he said with a twinkle in his eye, smiling.

"Well then Arnold, I guess you'll be in charge for a very long time, because I have no intention of getting my medical degree."

"And the entire medical profession thanks you for that decision." He laughed. "Come on, I'll walk you out. The girls will give you another appointment. I need to see you in a week and you'll need more blood work done. I'll make that appointment for tomorrow. I'll need those results as soon as possible."

With a look of consternation and concern splattered across my face, I timidly asked, "Why? Is there something you aren't telling me?"

"No. These were a little late arriving, through no fault of your own. Sometimes the labs get slammed. I guess this was one of those times. That's all."

"I'm happy that's all it was." I was relieved.

We said goodbye. I was on my way back to my family, my meds and the damn diet. Now, I had something new to add to the cauldron. I had to keep a journal. Will this *never* end?

I didn't know that Arnold had called Art, filling him in on exactly what my prognosis was, or in my case, was not. Art was to keep his own log of how he perceived my conditions and was encouraged to come along on my next appointment. Arnold had a sneaking suspicion that I wasn't telling either one precisely how I was feeling. So confronting me with Art's journal and Arnold's presence, I really couldn't escape. They'd have me exactly where they wanted me.

Confronting myself.

I was beyond ready to go back to the doctor. My pain was increasing in severity and I began noticing much more blood in the commode. I had no appetite and was so exhausted I could scarcely function. I refused to get on a scale to see how much weight I'd lost. There was no need. I could instantly tell by the way my clothes were hanging from my body. That told me everything I needed to know.

The only part of my body that hadn't lost weight was my face. It seemed to be getting fatter by the minute. It was the steroids I was taking, I would discover later. They gave me what doctors call a "moon face." If that wasn't bad enough, steroids also stimulate hair growth. For the hair on my head that was a really good thing. But, it didn't stop at my head.

Nope! Sadly it found its sneaky little way onto my face. Now, my normally smooth-skinned face had an unwelcome interloper. Please don't get me wrong. I wasn't becoming wolfgirl or anything. It wasn't as bad as that. But to me it might as well have been. I looked like the Pillsbury Dough Boy with a beard and really thick hair. Get the picture? Now you can see why it's a picture I'd much rather forget.

The only one who really seemed to notice this odd transformation was me. I had been looking at that face in the mirror my entire life, but the only thing I seemed to notice now, was someone else's face looking back. And, I didn't like it one bit. Hey, what do you expect!

I'm a girl and girls are prone to vanity. It's in our DNA.

On one of my vanity days, I was looking into the mirror and suddenly screeched, "Art! Quick! Get in here. You have to see this."

"What's wrong?" he asked, as fear gripped his heart like a cold hand.

"Look at my face."

"What in hell am I supposed to be looking for?" he asked.

"It's fat and hairy, for God's sake."

"Jesus, Carroll, you scared the hell out of me. Don't do that!" he said with a hint of annoyance. "It's round, that's all. We knew that would happen."

"Yes, but look at all the hair. It's everywhere!"

"It's not everywhere. It's just sorta fuzzy, that's all."

"Oh that's just great. So instead of looking like wolfman, I now look like Winnie the Pooh on steroids. A chubby little face stuck with fluffies, fuzzie wuzzie and all."

"At least you don't look like wolfman. Hell, I wouldn't be able to take you anywhere if you looked like him. You'd scare the hell out of everyone. But, Winnie? Now that's a whole different story. Everyone loves a cute cuddly fuzzy bear." Art couldn't stop laughing.

"Stop laughing. It's not funny."

"Yes it is; and quite frankly, you're being silly. You are a beautiful woman. Why do you refuse to see that? Do your friends run screaming when they see you?"

"Of course not," I answered.

"What about the kids?"

"No. They don't even notice. They're just. . . kids."

"But children are very perceptive. Perhaps, even more so than we realize. They love you. We all love you. You, my beautiful wife, should learn to love yourself, as well." Art took me into his arms as I began to sob.

"Maybe you're right. Maybe I am being silly."

"Of course I'm right. I'm always right."

"Smart ass," I said pinching his waist as I wiped away my tears.

He was right and I knew it. It was time to start acting more like a grownup and less like a child.

I had just been taught another of life's little lessons. Now I was about to tackle one more.

My trips to the market and other errands were definitely becoming a huge challenge for me. I hated going anywhere. Leaving the comfort and safety of my home these days had become a nightmare. Between the abdominal pain and the diarrhea, I'd been forced to discover the whereabouts of seemingly every bathroom in town. Unfortunately, on several occasions, I was compelled to make my acquaintance with many of them personally. Actually, it was more often than I cared to admit.

It was a most degrading and humbling experience. One which I would rather not have had, believe me. But like all warriors, I learned to sacrifice a little dignity for the sake of a bathroom stall.

In my bathroom journeys, I began noticing that all bathroom hygiene was definitely *not* created equal. In many cases, they were not fit to use. That really surprised me, because Barrington was a very upscale village. To have nearly unfit restrooms was, quite frankly, unconscionable. So I considered this as another learning experience, another of life's lessons I seemed to be learning nearly on a daily basis now.

That's how I began my education in turning lemons into lemonade. Not a big step, I know. But, someone once asked me, how do you eat an elephant? Just one bite at a time. I was ready to begin my new gourmet dining lessons on consuming elephants, one tiny bite at a time.

CHAPTER 5

I looked back at the Thanksgiving and Christmas of 1970 and won-dered how I managed to get through them. For the sake of every-one, I pretended to be having fun. Maybe if I pretended hard enough, I might actually feel better. Good food, great friends, and a loving family. They were my reasons for getting through a really tough time. I wasn't getting any better. My pain was becoming insufferable. So much more blood. More diarrhea. More nausea. But most of all, more denial. Yes, I was frantically attempting to will it all away. But my body was having none of it. It had other ideas for me.

Somehow, through it all, I still managed to keep a smile on my face and a positive upbeat attitude. I had to carry on with some semblance of normalcy in my home. The kind of normalcy I had before I was struck down by a disease we knew nothing about.

We were, however, about to learn just how unforgiving and terrify-ing my disease would become. My worst nightmare was about to be unveiled as the Sword of Domocles hung gprecariously above my head, simply waiting for instructions.

I hung on as long as possible until I could hang on no longer. In the first week of the New Year, January, 1971, everything changed. And it changed dramatically!

Art had just left home for O'Hare Airport and his flight west to Los Angeles. Somehow, those planes don't seem to be able to fly themselves.

I was getting Courtney ready for school, the baby was still sleeping, and Heidi had been fed. So far, just another normal day in the deCarle household.

Suddenly, I had to run to the bathroom and the closest one was just off the kitchen in our laundry room. I was doubled over with pain like I'd never encountered. Before I reached the bathroom I felt something warm running down my legs. I was certain my bladder had presented itself in a most unflattering manner. I was wrong. It wasn't my bladder at all. What was running down my leg was red. *Crimson!* By the time I sat on the commode I was shaking with fright and uncertainty.

"What was happening to me?" I cried knowing I needed help, but also knowing I had no way of reaching the phone. This was a time before cell or walk-around phones. I'm sure you can now appreciate my dilemma?

The only one in the house able to help, was a tiny five year old girl. More than anything, I detested what I was about to do.

"Courtney, honey, can you come in here for a minute?" I yelled in a voice trembling with guilt for having to place an enormous task on the shoulders of such a small child.

From around the corner peeked a little face. "Mummy, what's wrong? You don't look good." And then she began to cry. To this day, I can still see the fear in her eyes.

"Honey, mummy needs you to call Mary Ann and ask her to come quickly. Can you do that for me like a big girl?" I asked, scarcely able to get the words out while playing the role of my life pretending that it wasn't a big deal, but mummy still needed a grownup's help. "I have a really bad tummy ache and I feel like I'm going to throw up."

"Okay, mummy. I'll get the throw up bucket." Off she ran to her bathroom and her plastic bucket we kept there in case the kids needed it.

She returned, bucket in hand, asking, "are you gonna be alright, Mummy?"

"I'll be fine, honey, but please call Mary Ann for me, okay?"

Mary Ann arrived, took one look at me and realized I needed more than her help. I needed to be hospitalized.

"Courtney, why don't you get your things together and run next door. You and John can ride to school this morning. His daddy will drive you two, okay?" she said in a calm reassuring voice.

"Okay." Courtney answered as fear seemed to engulf her little body.

Mary Ann noticed the fear in Courtney's eyes and reminded her that I would be fine. "Mummy has a really bad tummy ache. I'm going to call her doctor and he'll come and make her better. So don't worry. Sometimes these things happen to moms and dads. She'll be just fine. You run along now. John's waiting for you and you don't want to be late for school."

"Okay. Get better Mum. Daddy will be home soon. I love you Mummy." She zipped up her parka, grabbed her lunch pail and headed next door.

Mary Ann called my doctor, explained what was happening as best she could. Arnold immediately made arrangements for an ambulance to take me to the Evanston Hospital. While we were awaiting its arrival, I had Mary Ann call my girlfriend, Bobbie, who agreed to come immediately to take over parenting until we could reach Art and get him home as quickly as possible.

Unfortunately, we learned from United's pilot scheduling desk that his plane had already departed for Los Angeles. They promised to get a message to him that it was an emergency and he would be met when his plane landed in Los Angeles. They were making arrangements to have him turn around and head back to Chicago. United had always been accommodating when it came to emergencies and this certainly was one of those times. Now, all I had left to do was try to remain calm and focused. Between the throwing up, the severe pain and all the blood, I was a mess. How in hell was I supposed to be calm? I was stuck sitting on the commode waiting for the ambulance to arrive holding a throw-up bucket in my lap while my friends paced nervously while attempting to keep me calm. It was taking so long for the ambulance to arrive. Why does it always feel like time stands still when there is a crisis? The hands of the clock seem to defy all logic in their quest for another minute. The waiting was endless and I had no idea how much longer I could hold on.

Aaah! Finally we heard the sirens as the ambulance approached our home. It was sweet music to my ears.

The paramedics had a difficult time stopping the bleeding long enough to get me off the commode and onto their gurney.

"Ma'am, how long has this bleeding been going on?" One of the paramedics asked shaking his head.

"I don't know. Maybe an hour." I answered through my pain.

Even they were shocked at the amount of blood in the toilet, on my legs, and on the floor. Nothing had been cleaned up per the instructions of my doctor. He wanted the paramedics to assess and report to him as soon as possible.

After being assured by my friends that they would take care of everything and not to worry, I was wheeled out of the laundry room while tears gushed from my eyes and great sobs wrenched my body. I was placed into the rear of the ambulance frightened to death and with lights and sirens, I was on my way. That hour in the ambulance was the longest trip of my life. They gave me something for the pain and continued working on me doing who knows what. But they were unable to give me something for the pain in my heart. I'd left my home in chaos, my daughter scared to death, my dog not knowing what all those people were doing in her home and my husband thousands of miles away unable to do anything until his plane landed back in Chicago.

Through all this confusion, a baby boy slept soundly in his crib completely oblivious to the happenings in the other end of the house. For that, I was very grateful.

CHAPTER 6

I stayed in the Evanston Hospital for nearly four weeks. When Art was home he made those long trips back and forth as often as possible. Our friends came to visit, as well.

Everyone was eager to pitch in to help Art through his chaotic new life as chief cook and bottle washer, chef, laundress, seamstress when necessary, cookie baker, ironer, popcorn popper, and a myriad of other duties. He was both mommy and daddy. He was becoming very proficient in tying little girl's bows, bathing two giggling kids, feeding one very large dog, braiding Courtney's hair, painting her fingernails and reading stories.

Doing little boy things was a natural. It didn't take much to please a thirteen month old. Changing diapers, keeping him supplied with plenty of stuffed animals and any vehicle with four wheels. All while attempting to keep him from riding on top of Heidi, or joining her in the pantry where they both gobbled Heidi's Milk Bones. That child loved to eat and wasn't all that particular as to what might be consumed. As long as it was food, it was fair game. It made absolutely no difference to Mac if he was helping Heidi eat hers or eating his own. As long as he had food he was one happy camper. He was truly his father's son. They both loved mealtime, except for the dog food part. Art wasn't ever going to be *that* hungry.

Art had to be exhausted at bedtime. Taking care of two little ones *was* exhausting. But he always seemed to be up to the challenge, never complaining.

After their baths and prayers, he would read a bedtime story, tell each he and mommy loved them very much, tuck them in, kiss them goodnight, turn out their lights and retire to the family room to sit and think.

Only then would he permit his fears and emotions to take hold. The doctors still had no idea what was wrong with me and that was taking its toll on everyone, not just me, but Art, perhaps even more so. He had to perform both fatherly and motherly duties, take care of the household accounts, fly his trips, and doing it all while worrying about me. I cannot begin to imagine the turmoil in his life.

In early February, 1971, my doctor sat down with Art telling him that there was only one thing left to do. I was only getting worse and if something else wasn't done and done quickly, I could quite possibly lose my battle.

"Art, if Carroll were my wife, I would have her at Mayo Clinic as quickly as possible. That's her last resort. Her body refuses to respond to any treatment. She's not going to win the battle if she continues on this downward spiral. And we don't want to even go there. To me, it's not an option. But, it's up to you, Art. It has to be your choice."

Stunned beyond belief, Art asked his friend, "Will you make the arrangements for me at Mayo Clinic? I'll get her there no matter what."

"I already have. I kinda knew what your decision would be. Pilots learn to make the right decisions, sometimes in a hell of a hurry. Rest assured, my friend, you have made the right one.

"In fact, I've been in constant contact with Mayo and before you leave here today, you'll have everything you need. All you'll have to concentrate on is getting her there as quickly as you can."

"Thanks for taking good care of both Carroll and me. How soon can you have her ready to leave here? I've got to make airline and hotel reservations and I have absolutely no idea where someone stays when up there. Got any ideas?"

"I have, actually. I had the people at both Mayo and Methodist Hospital, tell me which hotel would be best for you. It's the Kahler Hotel and it's connected to both Mayo and Methodist Hospital by a series of underground tunnels. At this time of the year the temperatures in Minnesota can be brutal. You'll appreciate those tunnels, I can assure you. But we'll need a day or so to get her ready to travel.

"And, Art, once she leaves here and spends a night at home, you've got to get her on the first plane out the next morning. I cannot stress that enough. I know how persuasive she is and how brave she pretends to be. Once she sees those kids and everyone as a whole family again, she'll try and con you into believing she really feels better. And she will, mentally. That's a good thing. But physically, whatever the hell is ravaging her body is killing her. Do you understand what I'm saying? It's that important that she be on the first plane out." Arnold was emphatic. It wasn't easy to tell his friend he could lose his wife.

"Shit!" Art said standing, running his hands through his hair, walking toward the window. Quietly, he stood there, looked out, but saw nothing. "Shit! Why Arnold? Why the hell her?" Turning with glistening eyes, he walked to his seat. "Why? Minnesota is such a long way from home. We know no one there. She'll be all alone when I can't be there."

"Believe me, Art, I've had plenty of time to observe her and that girl will adapt. She's strong willed, resilient as hell, has a great personality, and has three excellent reasons to get well. Two beautiful children and you. Oh, I think you underestimate her. She's got a helluva lot of moxy. She'll do just fine."

"God, I sure hope so. As long as she knows she'll be coming back home for good, she'll do great. Thanks. I feel a little better."

"You have to keep those positive thoughts in your mind. Don't for one second forget. You may need them and much more from which to draw strength," Arnold said, choosing his words carefully.

"What are you trying to tell me?" Art asked. His heart filled with dread.

"We have exhausted every resource available. Every doctor, everyone and everything, and still we're in the dark here. It's a goddamn mystery. What I'm about to tell you isn't going to be easy. You've got to prepare for the fact that she may not be coming back to us."

Silence engulfed the room. Suddenly Art said, "Shit! I feel like my heart just turned to ice. Like a thousand pound weight just dropped on my shoulders." A shiver slid up his spine as tears betrayed his eyes. He was frozen in his seat. "What in hell do I do?" Art asked, barely able to get the words out. "What do I do?"

"Right now, my friend, you sit there and get yourself together. Put a smile on that mug of yours and a helluva lot of hope in your heart because you and I are going to give Carroll the news together. I'll send my nurse in with some coffee. Black right?"

All Art could manage was a vacant look and an anemic nod of his head.

"Drink your coffee and I'll be back shortly. Okay?"

"Sure. Whatever," Art answered.

Arnold left and his nurse arrived with a carafe of coffee and two cups. Art poured himself a cup, desperately trying to wrap his head around what he'd just heard. He didn't know how to process everything thrown at him, and all at once. *How in hell am I supposed to handle this? I have no answers. Shit, no one has any answers. I'm gonna have to stumble through blindly navigating by the seat of my damn pants.*

When Arnold returned, Art was ready. "I pushed what you scared the shit out of me with to the back of my mind. That's where it'll stay. I promise you she will return to us. I know it. I just know it."

"Keep thinking that way and don't be afraid to ask God for His help. I know I do. In fact, I ask for His help a lot. Now, are we ready to go?"

"I'm ready. Let's get this over with."

"Art, let me do the talking. No mention of the part you're having difficulty with. Okay?"

"Jesus, Arnold! I'd never do that."

"I know. I'm just making sure, that's all."

"I'm so excited about going home." Carroll said with a trill of excitement in her voice. "I can hardly wait to see the kids and Heidi. God, I've been gone for so long I'm not sure they'll recognize me."

"I don't think you'll have to worry about that. They're bouncing like balls just waiting 'til you walk through the door."

Art watched as Carroll reveled in the news, talking incessantly about going home. But never, for a moment, forgetting what Arnold had told him about not allowing her to hoodwink him into staying home a few more days.

"Remember, you are only home for a day. Not two. Not three. But one . . . and only one." Art cautioned. "In the morning we are on a plane and on our way to Mayo Clinic. Like it or not, when we get to O'Hare you *will* be put in a wheelchair. I'm taking no chances. Is that understood my stubborn wife?"

"Understood, my bossy husband, but only because I have no energy. That's all."

"Right." He smiled.

No sense in disagreeing. I was already trying too hard to alleviate both our fears by pretending I was feeling a little better. Nearly as much as Art was pretending his heart wasn't breaking on a daily basis. I felt as though the proverbial silver lining had been ripped away from my life leaving nothing but dark clouds.

Our friend Bobbie spent the night to be there when we left early the next morning and to be there when the kids woke. Thank God for such unbelievably giving and loving friends.

CHAPTER 7

Icouldn't be going to a better hospital. Mayo Clinic was the most advanced hospital in the world. In fact, people traveled from every corner of the globe to be treated by the best of the best. I knew once I got settled, I would be in very capable hands, and Art would finally be able to relax a little. Plus, Arnold promised to keep him posted as well as the medical teams at Mayo. So you might say we were both in very good hands.

We arrived the next morning at the Rochester, Minnesota Airport. I was exhausted and didn't feel very well. We took one of the air sickness bags with us in case I needed to use it in the cab on our way to Mayo. Deciding to use a wheelchair was a godsend.

Art really looked exhausted, too. He had to be. He'd been stretched in a hundred directions and much of the time, all at once.

Getting away from everything for few days to fly his trips was good for him. It gave him something other than me and his disrupted home life to think about. It must have been like a breath of fresh air, until he arrived home and began the rat race all over again.

I wasn't sure which was worse. The pain I was experiencing or the pain I was causing everyone. I was racked with guilt and it was understandable. But I also knew there wasn't a damn thing I could do about it except get better and get home where I belonged to a family who needed me. Who loved me.

My days at Mayo's Methodist Hospital turned into weeks, which turned into months. It was determined that I did *not* have colitis, but something called Crohn's disease, a relatively unknown and rarely diagnosed disease.

For those of you who have never heard of Crohn's disease or have and really have no idea what it is, I'm going to explain it to you. It's not a glamorous disease, not that any disease is, but this one in particular drags with it some pretty stinky connotations. Something no one wants to talk about. At least not in public, nor in mixed company. If you guessed the one word that defines Crohn's, the one with a never-ending stigma attached to it, and you guessed *poop*, then you guessed correctly.

Now that we've skated past the obvious, it's time to move along. I'm going to explain what Crohn's disease is, and is not, so you'll have a working knowledge of how to best help someone you may know or love who is faced with this horrible and incurable disease.

Crohn's disease is considered an inflammatory bowel disease (IBD). The disease is characterized by periods of activity (out of remission) and inactivity (in remission). Remission is where you want to be.

Crohn's is a chronic incurable disorder which causes inflammation or ulceration of the digestive tract. The most common area affected by Crohn's is the section of the digestive tract called the ileum (end of the small intestine that joins the large intestine) and the large intestine (colon). Inflammation can also occur anywhere in the gastrointestinal (GI) tract from the mouth to the anus. Crohn's disease affects all layers of the intestinal walls causing ulcers. It can also spawn openings called fistulas. These fistulas usually occur around the rectal area and sometimes drain mucus or pus. Yes, I know, you're probably saying to yourself right about now, *toooo* much information. But bear with me; it's going to be easy to understand.

The severity of Crohn's varies greatly between individuals. Many people have only mild symptoms while others can have complications that in rare cases, can be life-threatening. Like me, for instance.

The inflammation caused by the disease sometimes affects the intestine's ability to absorb nutrients from food. This can lead to deficiencies in important vitamins including B12 and Folic Acid. Crohn's can increase the risk of kidney stones, gallstones, and various forms of anemia (decrease in amount of hemoglobin in red blood cells), cancer, heart disease, deep vein thrombosis, arthritis, and a host of others. The medications you are required to take will, in time, do irreparable damage to your body leaving you with a severely compromised immune system. This I know firsthand.

There is no known cure for Crohn's disease. This one sentence is what has defined my entire life, thus far. **NO CURE!!**

You cannot begin to imagine the full force of the impact of hearing those two little words. It stunned me. But I couldn't give up. Surely one day, some researcher somewhere, would find a cure. That was the hope that kept me going. The fuel in my engine.

Forty years later, there's still no advancement in the way of curing. Sure, there are new medicines for the treatment of Crohn's and there's also the second alternative, surgery. Both are a means used to control the disease with a goal to keep the patient in a state of remission. But still . . . no cure.

I fit into the surgery group. I've had numerous surgeries over the years, and fully expect to have more. Right now, I'm in remission. But the entire year of 2011, I was battling pain trying everything to get back into remission. That was a very long road.

The statistics on the estimated number of people in the United States affected by Crohn's is around 780,000 and around 907,000 with colitis. That's a whopping 1.6 million people. As many as 70,000 new cases yearly in the USA. And, oh yeah, in case you're interested, Crohn's is an equal opportunity disorder affecting men and women equally, although some statistics show women as having a slightly higher risk.

People of European (Caucasian) and Jewish decent are four to five times more likely to be diagnosed than other ethnic groups. Rates among those of Hispanic and Asian descent are lower than those of European and African heritage. Other factors seem to play a part in causing higher rates, including living in urban areas and living in northern climates. People of the industrialized nations of North America and Europe also have higher rates.

Crohn's can be diagnosed at any age, but most commonly during adolescence and early adulthood, typically between the ages of fifteen and thirty-five. The disease is rare before the age of eight and affects slightly more boys than girls. There are potentially 100,000 plus children under the age of 18 in the U.S. suffering from an IBD.

There appears to be a genetic link as the disease is more common in those having relatives with Crohn's. Approximately 20% of those diagnosed have a blood relative with an IBD. If that relative is a sibling, then the risk of developing Crohn's is thirty times higher than the general public. And rates are higher in smokers than non-smokers.

The cause of Crohn's disease is still unknown. In fact, it wasn't until 1932 that an American gastroenterologist, Dr. Burril Bernard Crohn, first described the unknown disease along with his two colleagues, Dr. Leon Ginzburg and Dr. Gordon D. Oppenheimer.

One of the most popular theories is that in a patient with Crohn's the immune system reacts abnormally mistaking bacteria, an unknown virus, or other substance occurring in the bowel, as being a foreign invader. The immune system's job is to attack and remove these *foreign* objects. This causes an increase in white blood cells in the lining of the intestines which leads to the inflammation associated with Crohn's.

Once the immune system has been *turned on*, the message to switch it off appears to not be thrown causing your body to attack itself.

Some scientists theorize the disease may be caused by infection or diet. To date there has been no evidence to those theories.

Although once thought to be a factor, research has ruled out stress, tension, and anxiety as causes for an IBD. Stress and anxiety are *not* the cause of Crohn's, but high levels of either may aggravate symptoms.

And in case you are asking yourself, "is Crohn's disease contagious?" The answer is unequivocally, **NO.** It is not contagious.

CHAPTER 8

Today most people have heard of Crohn's disease, but in 1971 it was still a mystery. In fact, for years doctors had been treating me off and on for colitis. Right church, wrong pew. However, the treatments are entirely different, or certainly were at that time.

At least now we had some of the mystery solved, but the big part was yet to be determined and you cannot imagine the battery of tests which were conducted on my poor sick body. Mayo is nothing if not thorough, I'll say that.

As you might imagine, my days there were long and lonely ones, except for the positive thinking books by both Reverend Robert Schuller and Reverend Norman Vincent Peale. Without those to read, underlining meaningful passages, and really beginning to understand the Power of Positive Thinking, I'm not certain I would have come through that dark period of my life.

My happiest days were when Art came to visit and the times I talked to my children and friends via phone. The medical staff was exceptionally kind, making sure I was well-taken care of, as were those who took great pride in seeing that my room was spotless, the windows sparkling clean so my view of the trees and sky would never be impeded by smudges. I was lonely, yes. But I was never alone.

The way the medical floor was laid out reminded me of a wheel. The circular nurse's station was the hub and the patient rooms jutting from the hub were the spokes. Ingenious really. I had never seen that layout of a hospital before.

My room was a private one for which I was truly grateful. I was battling my own demons and I neither wanted nor needed to entertain anyone else's.

One day I had an episode in the bathroom which changed the dynamics in one heck of a hurry. I discovered an enormous amount of blood and fecal matter coming from places it should not have. I couldn't tell where it was coming from; and quite frankly, I didn't care because it scared the hell out of me.

I pushed the emergency call button in the bathroom sending nurses immediately. They got me back to bed, called my doctor and a team arrived giving me something for severe pain.

They began their quest for yet more answers. I was glad that Art was still here, though he had to fly out that evening

I learned that at Mayo, you didn't have "a" doctor. You had a *team* of doctors headed by a chief doctor. In the beginning, it was a little bit overwhelming. But like anything else, you adapted, grateful for their expertise.

After stabilizing me and leaving to discuss their options, the doctors returned with news of what had to be done. It was a unanimous decision on their part. There was only one thing left that would save my life. An operation called an ileostomy. Art and I looked at one another having no idea what they were talking about.

"What is an ileostomy?" I asked. "I've never heard of such a thing. But then, I'd also never heard of Crohn's disease which you said I was suffering from. Please explain?" I asked frowning and confused. "And, please, no sugarcoating. I want to know everything."

Dr. Beahrs explained. "An ileostomy is an opening in the belly (abdominal wall) that is made during surgery. The end of the ileum (the lowest part of the small intestine) is brought through this opening to form a stoma, usually on the lower right side of the abdomen.

"When you look at your stoma, you are actually looking at the lining (the mucosa) of your small intestine, which looks a lot alike the lining of your cheek

"Unlike the anus, the stoma has no valve or shut-off muscle. This means you will not be able to control the passage of stool from the stoma. There are no nerve endings in the stoma, so the stoma itself is not a source of pain or discomfort.

"As part of this surgery, the colon (large intestine) and rectum (the lowest portion of colon where formed stool is held until passed out of the body through the anus) are often removed (this is called a colectomy). This means that the normal colon and rectum functions are no longer present. Sometimes, only part of the colon and rectum are removed."

He couldn't help but notice the vacant look on my face and knew that I was trying desperately to comprehend what in God's name this man was trying to tell me.

"I know it's a lot to take in, but if you'll allow me to continue, I might answer some of the questions that you want to ask. And when I'm finished, I'll leave you with some pamphlets for you to peruse on your own. Hearing it once is far from enough. But the ability to read and discuss with Art, between the two of you, I think you'll get the picture and see it more clearly.

Okay?"

"Yes. Please doctor, go on," Art answered.

"Okay. After the colon and rectum are removed or bypassed, waste no longer comes out of the body through the rectum and anus. Digestive contents now leave the body through the stoma. The drainage is collected in a pouch that sticks to the skin around the stoma. The pouch is fitted to you personally. It is working at all times and can be emptied as needed. The ileostomy output will be liquid to pasty, depending on what you eat, your meds, and other factors. Because the output is constant, you will need to empty the pouch five to eight times a day.

"The major job of your small intestine is to absorb nutrients and water from what you eat and drink. Enzymes (chemicals made by the body to break down food) are released into the small intestine to break food into small particles so that proteins, carbs, fats, vitamins, and minerals can be taken into the body. These enzymes are also in the ileostomy output and can irritate the skin. This is why the skin around your stoma must always be protected. But, we'll get into all that after your surgery."

"But why do I have to have one." I asked bewildered. "Surely there must be some medicine I haven't had yet that could keep this under control.

"Carroll, in your case nothing has worked and we've tried everything. Unfortunately, your intestine is irreparably diseased and damaged, and we're just left with no other choice."

"Oh great!" I cried. "Just great!"

"I think this is more than enough for you to digest at the moment. I know you said not to sugarcoat what's about to happen to you, and I respect your wishes to know everything ahead of time. But, Carroll, until we get inside and see exactly what we're are dealing with, I think the best thing for you and Art to do is go over the pamphlets I'm leaving with you, write down anything that you don't understand and I'll be happy to answer any and all questions. But for now, let's not get ahead of ourselves until we know what we're up against. Okay?" He took my hand in both of his and squeezed it gently.

"You are absolutely right, doctor," Art said. "I think we have more than enough information to go over and discuss. We'll get through this. And that's the main thing. But, Doctor Gregory, I'm scheduled to leave later today. I've got to fly the day after tomorrow and have to make arrangements for the children and with the airline to have someone cover my trips. I guess what I'm asking is do I have time to do everything and still be back for Carroll's surgery?"

"We might be able to postpone surgery for four days. But, I must warn you that is by no means a guarantee. I hope you understand what I'm implying here. I'm hoping that will be sufficient enough time for you?" the doctor told Art.

"I guess it'll have to be."

"Remember Art, until after all the tests are completed, we really won't know what we're dealing with. But as soon as I know, you'll know. Until then we'll manage her pain and keep her comfortable. Don't you worry? Either of you. We're pretty good at what we do here at Mayo. That's why the difficult cases come here."

As he smiled, he squeezed my hand saying, "and you, my dear, are my problem child. So I intend to take particular care of you."

Dr. Beahrs shook Art's hand. "I'll let you get to making your arrangements while I begin making mine."

"I'll walk out with you, doctor. I have a few more questions."

When they were out of earshot, the doctor further explained about the ileostomy to Art.

"I had a feeling you weren't telling us everything about the surgery."

"You're right. I didn't want to get into anything else with Carroll; I could see she was having difficulty processing what I was saying.

"Care to explain it to me?" Art asked.

"Gladly," he said. "What I left out was explaining a little about the small and large intestine. The small intestine is the longest section of the digestive tract. It's about 20 feet long. The large intestine (colon) joins the small intestine where the ileum and cecum meet on the body's right side. It is about 5 to 6 feet long. When the large intestine is removed, you are at a greater risk for electrolyte imbalance. Diarrhea, vomiting, and a lot of sweating can increase this risk. Also dehydration is a serious concern. If you get dehydrated, you'll need to drink more fluids. To avoid dehydration, you should try to drink 8 to 10 eight-ounce glasses of fluid a day. If you have diarrhea, you may need more.

"Loss of appetite, drowsiness, and leg cramps may be signs of sodium loss. Fatigue, muscle weakness, and shortness of breath may be signs of potassium loss. All can be extremely dangerous and must be treated right away.

"Now you can see why I elected not to tell her any more." The doctor explained.

"I appreciate that. I guess I'd better get back in there or she'll start worrying about what we're discussing. And I don't want that." Art said, shaking the doctor's hand.

"Good idea," Dr. Beahrs said.

After Art and the doctors were gone, I began to cry.

"Why are you crying?" Art said, re-entering my room. "He said he'd take good care of you and get you well again. There's nothing to cry about, honey."

"I don't know. I'm so tired of being forever in a hospital. And, still I don't really know anything."

"Yes we do. We know you have Crohn's. We know you'll have surgery to correct things and eliminate all the pain. What I think you are is frightened and that's understandable."

"Yeah! I'm really going to be sexy with that, that, horrible thing hanging around my body." I was confused, angry, sad, and scared to death, as tears rolled down my cheeks. My heart broke like a fragile glass as I suddenly began to realize the extent of what the doctors were saying.

"Oh stop that. You're just being silly." Art said.

"No I'm not. What if the thing has to be permanent and I never get rid of it? What then? How could you love me looking like some circus sideshow freak? 'Come see a phenomenon. Girl who poops in a bag.'

Shit! Shit! Why me? Why did this have to happen to me?" I asked as I began sobbing like there was no tomorrow.

"Now you're just feeling sorry for yourself and making no sense. First of all, they said it would probably be temporary. He was giving us all the scenarios. And if it isn't then so what, we'll deal with it. That appendage doesn't define who or what you are. I love you til death do us part. Through sickness and health. Did you forget those words? Honey, no matter what happens, I promise you we'll get through it. And we'll get through it with me at your side.

"And furthermore, you'd never make it in a sideshow. You're far too beautiful. So there." He said, kissing me and squeezing my hand.

"Maybe you're right." I said, half-heartedly.

"Of course I'm right. I'm always right, remember? I'm a guy. It's a guy thing. It's in our DNA." Art said, grinning. "Now get some rest. The nurse is here with your meds and I have some calls to make. Plus, I'm in desperate need of a cup of coffee. I'm going back to my room for awhile and I'll check in on you later before I leave for home. Okay?"

"Okay. I love you."

"I love you too. Get some rest."

Art stopped by the nurse's station to inform them of where he'd be.

"Don't worry about her, Mr. deCarle. We'll take good care of her. She's one of our favorite patients. She's quite a trooper, you know. She doesn't complain and is so grateful for the things we do to keep her comfy. Wish all our patients were like her. We just wanted you to know that you have a very special wife."

"Thank you for those kind words. You have no idea just how much they mean."

Later that day, Art left for home and I was left to myself to do far too much thinking. Not a good thing when you're about to face an uncertain surgery. But all I could do was think and pray. I did a lot of praying . . . A lot.

CHAPTER 9

Tuesday morning was proving to be just another morning. Art was home making necessary arrangements, when the phone rang. Suddenly, an uneasy feeling washed over him as he reached for the phone.

"Hello," Art managed while secretly feeling something was about to happen. And it wouldn't be good news.

"Mr. deCarle, it's Dr. Beahrs, I have scheduled Carroll for surgery on Friday morning. We've just looked over the results of her tests and it's a consensus of opinion that we cannot wait any longer. We discovered that the large intestine is extremely diseased. It also appears that a portion of the small bowel, may also be affected. But until we get in there and remove the intestines from the cavity and go over them thoroughly, we won't know just what we're up against."

"What's the worst case scenario?" Art asked, filled with a sense of dread.

"I wish I had a crystal ball, but I don't. The results could be any number of things. But I highly suspect she'll end up with a permanent ileostomy. I can't fathom repairing the amount of damage I'm seeing there. I don't know how in hell she's hung on this long. This is one of the worst cases I think I've ever encountered. That gal has one powerful constitution. That's all I have to say. But, it's imperative she keep that positive outlook. We'll do our part here, but you've got to do yours and keep reinforcing your love and support. She's gonna need it. For now, we'll prepare for the worst and pray for the best. Do you have any questions?"

"I'm sure I have many. Right now, I'm too stunned to think of any to ask."

"You have my number. Call anytime; and Mr. deCarle, I'm sure I don't have to remind you not to mention any of this to Carroll. She's battling enough demons right now. She sure as hell doesn't need any more. I'll keep your local doctor up to date.   I understand he's your friend. Don't hesitate to lean on him."

After hanging up, Art just sat there. His mind was traveling in every direction.

"Shit! When she hears this news she's gonna fall apart. And I can't leave here 'til Thursday. I hope her parents come early enough tomorrow. At least I'll have time to get them acquainted with the house, the kid's routine, and introduce them to George and Bobbie before I leave early Thursday morning for Mayo."

Art walked around the kitchen, mumbling. "This place is so empty without Carroll and the kids roaming about. With Courtney at school and Mac still sleeping, it looks like just you and me girl." Art said as he scratched Heidi and kissed her head. As he walked about muttering, Heidi laid there and just watched him as though she sensed he was hurting. Art finally plopped down on the family room couch and Heidi followed standing at attention like a soldier protecting her troops.

"Oh, Heidi, what are we going to do if mommy doesn't come back home?" Art said, rubbing Heidi's head. She knew something was wrong. Her mom wasn't here anymore and she was being shuttled back and forth with the kids to another house.

Yes, animals sense things, perhaps even more so than most people. Heidi knew Art was hurting. At that moment Heidi jumped up onto the couch, which she'd never done before, and placed her head in Art's lap refusing to leave his side.

Out loud, Art said, "What am I going to do, girl? What am I going to do?" Heidi made a sound like a moan and looked up at her master. "I know Heidi, you miss her too. God bless George and Bobbie, though, right? Had it not been for their generosity in taking you guys into their home, I don't know what in hell I would have done." Heidi nuzzled up closer to Art. "They drive Courtney to and from school five days a week, which means two round trips from their home to Barrington. What kind of person does that? Shit, the trip's at least forty-five minutes each way. More during rush hour. Those two are a gift from God. They're incredible friends. I cannot imagine what an upheaval it must be having the three of you, their own three, their dog, and all in their small home. Plus, Mac's still in diapers. What a job? How in hell they do it I'll never know. Yes, I guess I do know. They do it with love. So much love. They are the quintessential definition of the meaning *friend.*" Art scratched Heidi and kissed her snout. "I hope you know just how lucky you are, girl?" Art stood up. "Come on, girl, let's go out once more before we get Mac up, okay?" Heidi jumped off the couch and headed to the family room sliders. Art opened them and out she went. Art stood watching until she was finished with her business and whistled her back inside.

"Good girl. Let's get your breakfast. I'll bet you're hungry, aren't you?" Heidi ran to the laundry room, returned with her bowl in her mouth, deposited it at Art's feet, and barked.

This was going to be a very long day. And it had barely begun.

CHAPTER 10

Wednesday came and with it the excitement of my parents' arrival. My phone rang and it was Art calling.

"Hi!" I said. "Did they get there, yet?"

"Not yet. After you called them on Sunday and asked for their help, they called me and said they'd be driving. So I'll stick around here til they arrive. I have to do some laundry and finish packing. My flight leaves early tomorrow morning. I'll be up there in plenty of time. I've already checked the weather and no snow in sight here or there. That's good."

"I can't wait to see you. I've missed you, honey."

"Me, too. But now I have two jumping beans here who want to say hello."

"Hi Mummy," Courtney squealed into the phone. "Gramma and Grampa are coming today."

"Hi sweetie. I know they are. Are you excited?"

"Yes, yes. I am. I told Mac, but he's too little to understand. But, I told Heidi and she's very happy."

"I'll bet she is. She's a big girl so she understands those things. Make sure you have Heidi mind her manners while they're there. Okay? Sometimes doggies forget. Just like big sisters and little brothers."

"Okay, Mummy. We miss you. Hurry up and get better. You make better cookies than Daddy does," she whispered into the phone. "Wanna talk to Mac? Remember, he's just a baby and he doesn't know a lot of words."

"I'll remember. Thanks for reminding me, honey." I had to pull the phone away from my ear as she screeched, "Mac. Hurry up it's Mummy. She wants to talk to you."

I suddenly heard a tiny voice, saying, "Hi, Mummy!" Tears ran down my cheeks.

"Hi, Mac. Daddy tells me you are starting to walk now like a big boy."

"Big boy," he said quietly.

I had to giggle as he began talking a mile a minute. I picked out a few words that were distinguishable amidst his rambling.

"I love you, my baby boy. Now will you put Daddy back on the phone?"

"No baby, Mummy. I a big boy."

"I'm sorry. You are a really big boy now. I forgot. Put Daddy on, okay?"

"K. Bye, bye, Mummy."

"Bye, bye, darling."

In the background, I heard Courtney yelling, "bye, Mum."

"I'm back," Art said. "They're real chatter boxes, aren't they?"

"Oh, yes. I'll let you go now, and call when my parents arrive, okay?"

"Stop worrying. I said I'd call and I will. I promise. Now try and get some rest. Call you later, babe. Love ya."

"Love you too. Bye, hon."

I lay in my bed, alone and scared to death while thinking how Art's life had been stretched to nearly the breaking point. Between his occupation as an airline pilot, flying all over the country, and his duties as a husband and father of two little ones and a big dog, I knew he had to have been exhausted. And after arriving home to an empty house, unpacking, repacking, driving back to O'Hare to board yet another flight to Rochester, renting a car and driving to the Kahler Hotel, checking in, unpacking, and walking from the hotel through the underground tunnels leading to the Methodist Hospital and finally arriving at my bedside, I really didn't know why he wasn't walking on his knees. I was exhausted just thinking of everything he had been doing just to keep our family intact. Including his sanity.

I wasn't the only one affected by my disease. No, it had affected many people besides just me. This unknown element, which so abruptly entered my life, refused to leave, and was about to alter my life's dynamics *forever*.

Chapter 11

Alone in my bed thinking of all my yesterdays, praying for my tomorrows, Art was home all day with two little ones he had seen so seldom these past months. Home waiting for my parents who'd promised to come and help lift the burden of taking care of a small girl, a baby boy, and a dog. This should have been a relatively simple course of events for them. They were retired and had nothing important to monopolize their days. Doing this should be pretty easy. They didn't have to worry about housekeeping, laundry, or ironing, as I had a woman three days a week for that. All they needed to do was enjoy their grandkids.

It would also lift the burden from the shoulders of our friends who openly extended their home, their family, and their lives to our children and our dog. Never was a truer statement made than this one, "You can pick your friends, but you cannot pick your family." I was about to learn how true that statement would prove to be.

When my little family was in the care of George and Bobbie, I never once worried about how they were doing. I knew they were well taken care of and loved. My concerns were of a different nature. Would I ever hold them in my arms again? Would I see their smiling, happy little faces? Feel their warm, sweet breath upon my lips as I tucked them into bed and kissed them goodnight? I had already missed my baby's first words, his first steps. Would I be around to hear the sounds of laughter and squeals of delight as they learned to ride a bike without their training wheels? To watch Mac learn to swim in the lake. To see them graduate high school and college, and to be there when they were married. When they had their first child.

And through all my *would I's*, throughout their lives, one very important one haunted me. Would I be there to watch the evolution of their lives from a cocoon to caterpillar, and finally the emergence of a beautiful, graceful, and strong butterfly? A butterfly, which in the adversity of powerful headwinds, still manages to fly.

What kind of person would each grow to be? What events and values would help shape their lives? My only wish would be for them to be happy, loving, understanding, patient, and generous individuals, willing to pay their life's blessings and fortunes forward.

It's those thin threads we come upon and pull that make up the tapestry of our lives. Unopened doors which may provide answers to questions yet asked. Those unclaimed mysteries of life. Those *why's* which for most, unfortunately, may never be answered.

Art busied himself all day, just waiting for a call which never came. My parents had neither called nor had they yet arrived.

I lay in my hospital bed waiting to hear from Art. A call that would lift a thousand pounds of pressure from my very frail frame.

Sickness had ravaged my 5'9" frame; reducing it to a fragile weight of barely a hundred pounds. Praying for a miracle that would stop this train wreck from happening and not wanting to accept the words I heard yesterday from a team of unsmiling faces who'd entered my room. Their news was grim at best. My Crohn's disease was spreading rapidly through my intestinal tract. Until they went in and saw firsthand the damage already done, they could not predict an outcome. Not a real positive one, at least.

So there I was. Alone. Afraid. And asking, "Why me?"

The doctors had already informed Art of the severity of the situation, suggesting he get here as soon as possible. Friday they would operate. Time was of the essence.

I waited impatiently all day for a phone call from Art regarding my parents. At 7P.M. the phone finally rang. I was so relieved.

I quickly picked up the receiver, saying "Thank God. They're finally there." However, that was not the news I heard.

"I'm sorry, honey. I don't know how to tell you this, but not only are they *not* coming, they didn't even have the decency to call and tell me. They made me wait until I couldn't wait any longer and finally had to call them."

My heart nearly stopped beating at hearing his words. I cannot begin to explain the range of emotions I was experiencing at that moment.

"What do you mean they're not coming? Are they sick? Did they have an accident? Tell me they're okay?

"They're not sick and they didn't have an accident. They just aren't coming. That's all I can tell you." Art's voice was filled with pain as he delivered this news to me.

"Dear God, what do we do? My poor babies. I'm their mother and there's nothing I can do." I was sure I would never stop the tears from flowing. They were like a raging river rushing through a canyon. Through my tears and my outburst of sorrow, I suddenly heard Art's voice.

"Hey. Hey! Stop the tears. I've got things under control here. George and Bobbie are on their way. They're taking the kids and Heidi back with them. They send their love and they don't want you to worry about a thing. Okay?"

"Okay, but . . . why aren't' my parents coming? I don't understand this. I'm their daughter. My mother was a nurse. She must have some idea of this disease. Why, Art? Please tell me you have an answer for me? Please!" I cried.

"I'm sorry, Carroll. I can't answer that question, because they had no answer for me when I asked it. I told them to forget it, we'd make other arrangements. And then I hung up without saying another word."

"No! No, no, no. No one could be that calloused. Especially parents. What should I think? Please tell me." I cried uncontrollably into the phone.

"I can't. I have no answers. I'm stunned as much as you are. The only thing to do now is get my ass in gear and get on the first plane tomorrow. Unfortunately, there are no more flights tonight. I've already made reservations with North Central, the Kahler Hotel, and the car rental agency. Thank goodness for the tunnels running from the hotel to the hospital. It's pretty cold up there."

"But, Art, my surgery is this Friday morning and you might not be here in time. Oh, no. What will I do?" Again the dam burst and tears flooded the canyon.

"Stop crying and listen to me. Please, honey."

Through my tears I managed to mumble, "I'm listening."

"Good. I've talked to your doctor and explained everything and he assured me they would hold off your surgery until I arrived. I'll be there in plenty of time. I promise. Alright?"

"Alright."

"He assured me that you would have enough medication to keep your pain under control. Are you hearing me? If you are nodding, remember, I can't see you. You actually have to speak."

"Sorry. I guess I was nodding." A slight smile crossed my lips. Art always knew the right things to say to reassure me. Why was I so lucky to have this man in my life?

"Are you okay?" Art asked.

"No. But I promise I will be after you get here."

"Try and rest and not worry. Bury the mess with your parents in some place deep and leave it there. It will do you no good at all to resurrect it. I'm sure it's difficult, but nevertheless, you have to go into this surgery with a positive frame of mind."

"I'll try."

"Don't try. Just do it. Keep reading those books I gave you by Robert Schuller and Norman Vincent Peale. They'll get you through tough days ahead. Okay?"

"I have been. Those books, those words, all the love and support from you, the kids, and our friends, are my life's blood for surviving this thing."

"Good girl. I miss you, honey, and I love you. Everyone sends their love and best wishes."

"I love you, Art. I miss you and I need you."

"You have me. All of me. Now get some rest. I'll see you tomorrow."

We blew kisses across the phone lines as we said our goodnights.

After hanging up, I cried and cried until there were no tears left. I decided at that moment, I would not allow anyone to control my life. Taking pen in hand, I wrote a scathing letter to my parents. It would be the last conversation I would have with them. They would never disrupt my life nor that of my family ever again. Art and the kids were the most important things in my life. The mere fact that they didn't come, didn't have the decency to call to say they weren't coming, and even had the unmitigated gall to keep Art waiting all day long, placing him in an awkward position of having to call them, was unfathomable to me. I can only imagine his surprise when my mother answered the phone and told him they were not coming. Art was livid, to say the least. He had to make new arrangements with George and Bobbie. And then he had the difficult job of calling and telling me that my own parents were a no-show. There actions were unconscionable and reprehensible. Did they care so little about me that it meant nothing to them at all?

I ended my letter by writing "Do not ever write or call again. I will survive. I will go on.

And my family will do it as a loving, cohesive unit. Without you in it."

I sealed, stamped it, and gave it to the nurse to post for me. I knew I would get a response from my mother. I knew her well enough to know she couldn't let it go, needing to have the last word and she would never apologize for her actions. And yes, I did receive a letter a few weeks later from her. When I saw the writing on the envelope, I knew immediately who it was from. I ripped it up and discarded in the trash can. Just the way they'd discarded me.

To this day, I have no idea what was in that letter, nor do I care. My parents would never have an opportunity to hurt my family or disrupt our lives again.

Like they say, "You can pick your friends, but you can't pick you family." My friends *are* my family. And may God bless them all.

Later, that evening, I rang for my nurse asking if she would kindly fetch the chaplain.

"Carroll, what happened?" Barb asked, genuinely concerned.

"My parents didn't come." I began crying again as she sat on my bed holding my hand and allowing me to cry and talk and cry until I was all cried and talked out.

"I'm so sorry, Carroll. I know how much you were depending on them. But as odd as what I'm about to say might sound, I want you to keep remembering it. I have a profoundly deep faith in my Lord Jesus Christ. He has guided me through some tumultuous times in my life. I know you believe in Him as well. I know this from the long conversations we've had. Right?"

"Yes . . . yes," I said, trying desperately to regain some composure.

"Don't give up believing in Him. He'll never give up believing in you. Times like now you are being tested and it's so much simpler to just give up. It's natural. We all do it. But, now more than ever, you need to stay positive and connected to God. He won't let you down. He never lets us down."

"Then why is He doing this to us? I don't understand."

"And maybe you never will. But, it is His plan. By doing the things He does, He's making us choose. Do I give up and give in to adversity? Or do I dig in and press on to better days. You can, and probably will, ask yourself many times throughout your life, *Why? Why me?* Someday your *Why* may be answered, if fortunate enough. But, if it is answered, it may not be the answer you were hoping for. But trust me, within that answer will be your quest for something greater. Be open and accepting and you'll be rewarded ten fold."

"How do you know these things? How can you be so sure? I don't understand."

"You don't need to understand. You just need to believe. Allow Him to do all the worrying for you. He'll not let you down and He'll not forsake you. This I *can* promise you."

"Thank you, Barb. Thank you for everything. Somehow I feel lighter. I feel hope and I know I won't be abandoned."

She bent down and hugged me and in doing so I could feel her strength enter my body. I think she was sent to me by someone other than the person making out the nurses schedules. And you'll never convince me, otherwise.

Later that evening a minister arrived and I bared my soul. He made it so easy for me to talk, to listen and to hear. I'd discover later on that he was my nurse, Barbara's, pastor from her church. In the days, weeks, and months ahead, we would become good friends. He was someone Art got to know and like as well. He was a great comfort to us both.

After everyone left and I was alone with my thoughts, I decided that to effectively rid myself of what my parents did, I had to eradicate them completely from all thought and feeling.

At that moment I took all the negative events of the day, metaphorically placed them in a bottle, corked it and buried it far, far away. Never to be unearthed. This is one archeological dig I would *never* embark on. Many things in our past are meant to be buried and kept there forever.

This decision I made had to be executed in order to get me through what I was about to face. Believe me, I needed every ounce of strength, every positive thought, and all the loving help available to me. I was the architect of my own life and I would live it the way God had intended. With love, compassion, forgiveness, strength, and a joyful heart.

CHAPTER 12

It was Thursday morning, Holy Thursday to be exact, and I was already having a crappy day. It was driving me nuts that everyone around me was so upbeat and positive when I felt my life disintegrating before my very eyes. My body was decimated by some horrible disease which would never be cured. I was going to have to wear some god-awful bag that would forever be filled with poop while stuck to my belly til the end of time. And to think, while I watched as my shitty life slipped in a vortex down the toilet, the last thing anyone would ever remember was my fat, hairy, Pillsbury Dough Boy face.

"Shit! Shit! Shit!" I cried. "Why, God? Why me? You must know I have two little ones at home who need their mother to be whole. How can I possibly be whole with what I'm about to go through. I know you never give us more than we can handle, but don't you think you may have gone just a little overboard on me?" Tears rolled down my cheeks as I clutched a book by Rev. Schuller which Art had given me.

"Well, God, tomorrow I will face the worst day of my life. I am so scared. I have been unable to think clearly, feel clearly, or even speak clearly. I'm sick to my stomach knowing I may not come back to You or to my family. But please, God, allow me to return and give me the strength I'll need to tackle what's ahead of me. The vast unknown. I feel so alone, so utterly alone. I really hope you can hear me."

I lay in my bed all alone and hopelessly lost waiting for Art. I was in such pain I almost didn't care what happened to me. Between the vomiting, the diarrhea, and horrendous pain, I was slowly giving up. I'd just spent my last ounce of energy asking God for His help. There was nothing more I could do.

Suddenly, something happened. My room grew eerily quiet. Curiously, I looked at my television and turned up the volume, but could hear nothing. Why? As I looked through the open doors of my room into a bustling busy hall, I was filled with a sense of uneasiness. Mouths were moving, which meant people were talking and moving about, yet, I could hear absolutely nothing. I became consumed by fear. My heart pounded so loudly, I could feel it in my ears.

"Dear God, now I've lost my hearing. It wasn't bad enough that I was throwing up, having diarrhea, and having such horrible pain, but now you've managed to take away my hearing. Why are you doing this to me? Why? I can't handle anything else. I can't. Why don't you spread this mess around and give some to others. I can't handle any more of this."

I began crying, but was unable to hear my own cries. An awful pessimism descended in my mind and I felt my insides freeze. I frantically reached for my call button, pushing wildly until someone came. But, no one did. Even when I cried aloud for help, no one heard. I lay there clutching my precious book tight to my breast. I closed my eyes hoping that when I opened them it all would have been a horrible nightmare.

But it wasn't. I hadn't been dreaming. It was really happening. I'd heard a thousand voices in my head, but was unable to understand their words.

To make matters worse, suddenly everything stopped. The television was motionless; there was no activity beyond my doorway. Everyone in the nurse's station was frozen. It was like time had stood still and the only one moving was me.

The sky grew dark and the temperature in my room grew frigid. Now, I was certain my worst fears had come true. I had just died. And, I'd died all alone.

"Why did you do this?" I cried. "Didn't I have enough problems? First you made me think I'd gone deaf, now you're making me think I'm dead. And you let me die by myself. Why, God? Why? It isn't supposed to be like this. Or is it? How would I know? I've never met anyone who's ever died and come back to tell me. You didn't even allow me to tell my husband and kids how much I loved them and how much I'm gonna miss them."

I thought I would throw up. I was left with a near-total absence of thought or hope. This frighteningly stranded, left-behind feeling, lingered.

All of a sudden, something bizarre happened. Something surreal touched my cheek. It was as light and delicate as a down feather. Softly and tenderly, someone or something whispered in my ear, *"ALL WILL BE WELL."*

As I touched my cheek, my eyes filled with tears, afraid to ask the question which begged to be asked. "Had I just been touched by the hand of God? Had He just whispered in my ear as He took me through heaven's gates?"

All I knew was that I wanted and needed to immortalize these feelings, these words, in my heart forever. I agreed to allow this emotional state to tower over all logic like a fool-hardy Goliath. I was left with a dizzy, powerful, positive feeling; as though my soul had miraculously been unchained. I had just experienced a paralyzing moment of sudden insight. Clarity, like the clarity of a stream fed by melting snow, it was absolutely crystal clear and real. *Very, very real.*

At that precise moment, the darkness lifted and drifted away. Faint sunshine once again shone through my window eager to illuminate my path ahead.

Yes, I was convinced that God had indeed whispered those four powerful words in my ear. Tomorrow when I went under the knife no matter what happened, what condition my body would be left in, I knew beyond all shadow of doubt, I would emerge whole again. I would go home once more to a family who needed me. As bleak as it all felt a short time ago, everything was back to normal. The television was back on and blaring. The sun was still shining. The noisy hustle and bustle of a hospital all back to normal and all music to my ears. Sweet, glorious music.

As I breathed a cleansing sigh of relief, my nurse popped in. "Carroll, I noticed your call button. Can I get you anything? Is everything alright?"

"I'm so sorry. I must have pressed it by mistake. Thank you for coming anyway."

"Anytime. You know that. But it's about time for your meds, so I'll be right back. We need to keep ahead of your pain until tomorrow."

"Thank you."

After she left, I turned and looked out the window toward the sky; the sun peered through a break in the clouds. Its light percolated through the dense tangle of pine bows on the trees just outside my window. I smiled through my tears and thanked God. I also apologized for everything I'd said to Him earlier regarding the dying thing. Heck, I wasn't going to die. He'd just promised me.

I don't know exactly what happened in my room that Thursday morning. All I know is something very special happened and it happened between me and God. People can dispel it as a hallucination as a result of the pain medication, or the ramblings of a sick woman grasping at anything. But they'll never convince me it was not the hand of God.

I'm here today when there was no hope for me. He believed in me even when I gave up believing in Him. I'll always believe in His power. I'll never doubt it.

Oh yes, I questioned "Why me"? So would you. I've asked myself that question many times throughout my life. More that forty years asking "Why me?" I had no answer. Maybe I wasn't supposed to. Or maybe it was God's way of making sure I remembered those days long ago when He visited me. I don't know. But when He's ready, He'll let me know. I only hope I'll be ready to hear what He has to tell me.

I think He chose me because I was to be part of a larger plan. We're all placed on this earth with a purpose. Mine was shown to me that cold day in March. He had bigger plans for me. I pray I'm wise enough to see them. To understand them. To fulfill them.

Chapter 13

Art arrived late Thursday morning, after my special moment had come and gone. He arrived with flowers and smiles and another little brown bottle with an artificial red rose to add to my growing collection standing at attention on my window sill. Small bottles of Lancers wine were given to North Central's passenger on their tray along with an artificial rose. Either a red rose or a yellow one. And, for some reason, I wanted to keep the empty little brown bottles and placed a rose in each one. I don't know why it was important to do that. Maybe to remind me of all the sacrifices Art, the kids, and my friends were making on my behalf. But, I do know that they served a very important purpose in my life. And yes, I still have a little brown bottle and a red rose tucked away in a box of mementoes.

Thursday was a particularly long day both physically and mentally. And I know it must have been a stressful one for Art, as well. He was trying so hard to keep my spirits up and my mind off of tomorrow morning. Even my nurses and candy stripers were especially bubbly. Or was it my imagination? No matter what it was, it was working.

This wasn't just any Thursday. No, it was Holy Thursday which made what had happened to me earlier, even more special. I don't know how many people have had the experience of having God speak to them. But for Him to do it on Holy Thursday was extraordinary.

I had told only two people of my miracle. My whisper from God. My special nurse, Barbara, and her pastor. No one else. Not even Art. This had been a private and pivotal moment in my life and I didn't want anyone saying it was probably a dream or the meds or simply pooh-poohing the whole thing. Not today. Not now. Now I was preparing for tomorrow's surgery. It would be successful and I would be back in this room with these wonderful people; my husband and my new friends. They would once again see the smile on my face and the light in my green eyes bearing witness to the fact that there was indeed a higher power.

Tomorrow was not just any Friday, either. It was Good Friday. Maybe this was an omen.

I still get a shiver up my spine when I think about it.

Art stayed until nearly eight-thirty P.M., before leaving to go back to his room at the Kahler Hotel. It was a cold, blustery winter day, threatening to snow. I was so relieved that Art was already here and not stuck in a snowstorm somewhere. Having the ability to go from the hospital through the underground tunnels to his hotel, was a blessing. Especially in bad weather.

My nurse, Barb, had informed me earlier that morning that she had taken Friday, Saturday, and Sunday off so she could be at my side before and after my surgery. When Art heard this he couldn't believe his ears. Why would someone take their few precious days off and spend them with a stranger.

He corralled her during the afternoon and privately offered to hire her for those three days. She flatly refused and wouldn't budge no matter how hard he'd tried. She told him that she and I had become much more than just nurse and patient. We had become friends. And this was something she wanted to do. She needed to do. It's what friends did for friends.

It was difficult for Art to fully understand such random acts of kindness by strangers. It was simply unbelievable. Yet it seemed to be happening all around him.

After my final preparations were completed for my morning surgery, I was given my meds. I silently, confidently, and peacefully fell asleep. I was content. I was ready. I was in the powerful hands of God. He would lead me through my darkest hour and into the light. Of this, I believed.

CHAPTER 14

Friday morning came early. But somehow in hospitals, mornings always seemed to arrive early. Like five A.M. early. This one was no exception. I was able to have a nice warm sponge bath and brush my teeth and hair and I felt so much better.

Yesterday, Art used a product called Minipoo Dry Shampoo, on my hair. He discovered it when he went to the pharmacy to see what they had for people who were unable to wash their hair.

It wasn't great, but at least my hair felt clean. I could hardly wait for the day when I could get a shower and scrub and scrub my hair with real shampoo. But until that day arrived, Minipoo was my new best friend.

Art arrived early this morning as he said he would. We talked and laughed while he tried desperately to keep my mind focused on anything but what was about to happen to me. He was doing an excellent job until my doctors walked in. At least they arrived with smiles on their faces accompanied by really positive attitudes. I think they were here more to see how I was doing mentally than to explain my procedure.

Before Dr. Beahrs and his team left, I said, "Doctor Gregory, would you do me a favor?"

"Certainly. What can I do?" A quizzical expression crossed his face.

"Will you silently pray with me?"

"I would be honored." He took one hand, Art the other, and we bowed our heads in silent prayer.

After our prayer, he squeezed my hand, saying. "I'll see you soon pretty lady." He smiled and left my room whistling.

I don't remember much about that morning, except for Art's continual banter as he tried to put up a strong front for my benefit.

Before they wheeled me out of my room we kissed, said our "I love you's" and I cried. Through my tears I managed to say, "I'll see you later. So don't wander off too far."

"I won't. But I think I'll get some breakfast and a lot of coffee." Smiling as he held my hand while they wheeled me out. I had to laugh at his reference to breakfast. That man loves to eat, yet never gains a pound.

"Don't mention food. It's been so long since I've actually used my teeth for chewing, I'm not sure they'll remember what they're for." We both laughed. Each attempting to put up a good front. Both trying so hard. So very hard.

Art walked along beside my golden chariot. Actually, it was my rolling bed, but somehow when Art called it my golden chariot, it felt less institutional and a heck of a lot more regal. I was shocked to see a cadre of nurses, doctors, maintenance people, and candy stripers, all clapping and wishing me well while being rolled toward the elevators. It was quite a sight. One I'll remember the rest of my life.

Art's journey ended as they rolled me into the elevator. I was glad my pain meds and whatever else they had given me in my IV, were beginning to take effect. I was drifting off to la la land and I really didn't want to think about anything else as the doors closed behind Art's smiling face.

I would see him soon. I believed that. That was the last thing I remembered just as I fell fast asleep.

Art had breakfast, returned to his room and attempted to take his mind off everything that was taking place in the operating room. His television and his novels only served their purpose for just so long.

"I can't sit here any longer." he said as he turned off the TV and picked up his novel. "I might as well go back to Carroll's room. She's all I can concentrate on now anyway." Art put his room key in his pocket and headed out the door and back to the hospital.

The doctors told him it would be a very long surgery. Little did he know just how long it would end up being.

He kept inquiring every hour or so until finally, nearly nine hours later, the nurse informed him that it was over and the surgeon would be by to speak with him.

When the Doctor Gregory finally entered the room, Art was petrified as to what he might tell him.

"How are you holding up Mr. deCarle?" he asked, while shaking Art's hand.

"I'm fine. But how is my wife. It took so damn long." Art said, raking his fingers through his hair.

"It took longer than I had hoped because the disease was *so* extensive. We had to remove all of her large intestine and a portion of her small one, her appendix and we sewed her rectum shut. There was a good deal of blood loss and she was given blood.

"She's been moved to critical care and we'll keep her there until I feel we can move her back here to her own room."

"Exactly what does all this mean?" Art asked

"She'll have a permanent ileostomy for the rest of her life. I'm sorry to have to give you that kind of news. However, the main thing is we were able to save her life. Don't ever forget that. She's still with us and that's a miracle.

"The only thing that's changed is the fact that she'll have to wear a pouch, and I have a feeling it won't be an easy transition for her. With women it's a cosmetic thing, more or less. Trust me; she won't look any different in her clothing.

"But let's not get ahead of ourselves. Let's concentrate on getting her strong again. That should be paramount right now."

"Of course. Can I see her now?" Art asked.

"In a little while. They're getting her situated in CCU, and when they've completed their duties, I'll have a nurse come and get you. Right now she's resting comfortably, but she'll have a great deal of pain. It's a bitch of an operation. I won't lie to you. It's the most painful operation there is. A seriously painful surgery. I had to make an incision from above the waist to the groin which constitutes cutting through the muscle wall of the abdomen. My concerns now are to get her through the first forty-eight hours. The most critical time for her. She was one very sick gal.

"Art, we have a chapel here. If you are so inclined, might I suggest you pay our chapel a visit. It will be good for you and for Carroll. She's going to need all the prayers and strength to get through this."

"Thanks, doctor. I think I'll do just that."

"I'll be around and I'll keep good tabs on our girl. Just let the nurses know where you'll be."

"Will do. And again, thank you."

They shook hands and Art made his way to the chapel thinking as he walked how exhausted Dr. Beahrs looked. He really looked spent. No wonder. Leaning over an operating table for nine hours, I'm surprised he's standing at all.

I was moved to ICU on Sunday morning. It wasn't just any old Sunday, it was Easter Sunday. Finally, off the critical list, out of CCU into ICU for a few days, I was looking forward to my own private room. I had days when I was a little more lucid than others, but for the most part, I was pretty much sedated the majority of the time. Those days were but a blur, a distant memory.

It wasn't until the following Sunday morning that I'd been moved to my own room. I remember opening my eyes trying to recall where I was and what'd happened to me. The thing that woke me was the sound of Rev. Schuller's voice. I was dreaming, surely. I had to have been. Right? Wrong. It was as though the pages of his book that I'd refused to let go of, had come to life. And actually, in an odd sort of way, perhaps they had.

CHAPTER 15

The weeks ahead were grueling ones. Having to simply move my body was a nightmare. Each time I took a breath, it hurt. The nurses tried to get me out of bed to sit in a chair and I fought them every inch of the way. My bed was my safe haven and I wasn't planning to venture from it.

One day, my doctor came to inform me that I had no choice in the matter. I had to get out of bed and sit in the chair. He was such a terrific man, that I was too embarrassed to tell him no. So, much to my annoyance, both he and my nurse helped me from my bed, to the chair, where I placed myself. Or rather, where they placed me. I was crying the entire time. The pain was horrific. But they gave me no choice. I had to do this if I ever wanted to get well again.

The first step was the chair. The next would be to take a few actual steps with a nurse on both sides for assistance. It all sounded pretty simple enough. But, I'm here to tell you it was pure hell. The pain . . . unbearable. My tears nearly unstoppable. I couldn't get my brain to inform my feet that they actually had to move. One foot in front of the other. They simply refused. Each time I cried "no." The nurses said, "yes." They never once allowed me to win. Those poor nurses dragged me, day after day, around my room. Toes scrapping along the floor until my slippers fell off one after the other. If my slippers had had metal toes surely sparks would be flying everywhere. Those feet of mine had a mind of their own and they were having none of this nonsense.

One day my brain finally fired on all cylinders and informed my feet to do their job. And, lo and behold, there I was moving at a snails pace, with the help of my nurses, but my feet were really moving . . . one size ten slipper at a time.

Gee, I was learning all sorts of tricks. First, sitting in a chair. And now, walking, albeit slowly; but nevertheless, still I was walking. My next feat was to attempt walking in an upright position. No, I wasn't crawling, but I was bent over. It hurt far too much to stand erect.

All these new and exciting lessons I was expected to learn and perform two to three times a day, were becoming a chore. Quite frankly, I was ready to strangle my nurses. Didn't they understand I was in pain? Didn't they care? I just wanted to be left alone to wallow in my self-pity. I was having my own pity party and I wanted no one else to attend. It was mine and I had no intention of sharing.

One day the nurse arrived and informed me that I would be going to physical therapy. "Physical Therapy?" I asked indignantly. "Don't you think I'm getting enough physical therapy walking all over the hospital and back? I'm not a guinea pig. You are not going to use me as some lab rat. Understood?"

"Yep, I understand. Now, Carroll they are going to wheel you to Physical Therapy and that's that. No more fussing. *Understood?*"

"Understood." I said reluctantly.

God, did these people have no compassion? There were days I felt as though I would die, and oftentimes, wished I had, the pain was so intense.

I was fully aware that everything I was learning to do was for my own benefit. My own well-being. Before I could even begin to think about going home, I had a lot of things to learn.

And I had to learn to do them alone. These would be my responsibility, only mine. However, I wasn't quite there yet. I still had a lot of hoops to jump through. And the biggest hurdle I had to leap over was the one involving my ileostomy. That would be the real test of my resolve.

For weeks they tried and tried to teach me how to take care of one simple thing. It was the first of many steps. It was imperative I take that first step, but I was unwilling. I even refused to look at that thing that would forever be attached to my belly. It was gross. But what was really the problem, was me. I was so afraid to look at my surgical site while the nurses managed it for me. I just wasn't ready to do that. I didn't know if I would ever be ready, quite frankly. I was the problem, not my ileostomy. It was doing fairly well all by itself. With the help of the nurses, that is.

Mentally, I was not ready to wrap my head around this thing. Secretly, I think in some convoluted crazy way of thinking, I really thought if I didn't actually acknowledge its presence, it would not be there. But, it was there and I knew it and it wasn't going to disappear no matter how hard I'd wished.

One day in April, the nurse was attempting to get me to do the changing of my appliance on my own. And I was, once again, balking, crying and annoying the hell out of her. Suddenly, in walked Art.

"What seems to be the problem, here? I could hear you out in the hall." he asked, already knowing the answer.

"They want me to change this thing and I don't want to. That's the problem." I said, pouting.

"How difficult can it be?" he asked the nurse

"It's not difficult at all. It just takes practice and that's what I'm trying to get Carroll to do. But she just won't try."

"I'll tell you what," Art offered. "Why don't you show me and allow me to do it for her. Just for now. And I promise she *will* do it the next time." he said, glaring at me and my childish behavior.

"Are you certain, Mr. deCarle? It has a tendency to get a little messy," she said, not quite sure he really knew what he'd be getting himself into.

"It can't be any messier than changing a baby's dirty diaper. I assure you, I've had my share of those. Now, show me what to do. I really need to know so I can help once we're home. And Carroll, stop your whining and pay attention. Because I can guarantee, you *will* do this the next time."

That was the day I took my first look at my ileostomy. I was in shock. It was a sight my mind refused to accept, but one I knew I'd never forget.

Art did a fabulous job his first try at changing my appliance. His hands didn't shake at all. I was really proud of him. And at the same time, I was really ashamed of me. My actions were that of a child, totally reprehensible. What was I thinking? Worse than what *I* was thinking, what must my nurses have been thinking of my childish behavior.

I obviously learned how to master the art of changing my own appliance, emptying its contents, and all without the aid of the nurses. Well, maybe not quite *mastering*, but I did finally get my hands to stop shaking like two lonely leaves on a windy day.

For now at least, both mind and body were on the same track going in the right direction. Before long, I knew I'd finally be going home.

HOME! Boy did that sound good. I hadn't been there since January. My children were growing up without me and I hated that.

CHAPTER 16

One day in early May, I was told I could go home. I was ecstatic. I was also terrified. I'd been here for so long with everyone doing everything for me. Safe, secure, and unafraid in my own little world. But that was about to end. Everything I'd once taken for granted was about to hit me dead-on. Was I strong enough to get through it all? Strong enough to pick up Mac? Yes, he's a baby, but right now he's probably a heck of a lot stronger than me. So many questions. So few answers.

How would I begin to manage without Art's help? He couldn't be there forever; he had a job, an airplane to fly, and I had a home and a family to run. Could I do it? I'd nearly forgotten how. So many doubts skirted the edges of my consciousness. Each quietly hidden behind the veil of uncertainty.

"Oh, no, here I go again. Miss Doubting Thomas. Get over it, Carroll. If you weren't ready to go home and do all the things a mother must do, within moderation, you would not be allowed to go. Think about it. The last thing they want is for you to have to come back here again." I said, sighing heavily. "Okay, Carroll. You can do this. You have no choice. Those little ones miss you and they need their Mum's happy, smiling face again. You owe it to them ... to all of them. Home is where you belong. So get over yourself and just do it!"

I unscrambled my scrambled brain and realized I wouldn't fall apart. My appliance would be okay. I now knew what to do with it when it was necessary. What I didn't know, however, and happy *that* I didn't know, was occasionally it will spring a leak at the most inopportune times; thus, creating some of my most embarrassing moments. It was also times like those which made me a stronger person while teaching me to turn those stumbling blocks into building blocks and go from there. Providing, however, we're smart enough to learn. Thank God,

I was smart enough to learn what to do when an accident happened. I was always prepared when I left home to have backup supplies.

My doctor sat behind his desk and smiled, saying, "Carroll, you're finally going home." Art squeezed my hand, looked at me and beamed.

"However, I have one very important task left for you to do. One final hurdle to get over."

I looked at him in bewilderment, thinking, *you've got to be kidding!!*

"You both have to spend the night in Art's room at the Kahler before I'll release you."

I asked, with a hint of confusion in my voice, "What's so important about that?"

"You'll spend the night in the same bed, making love as you'd normally do and then report to me in the morning. Both of you."

"Let me see if I'm getting this," I said, with a hint of sarcasm. "You're telling me I have to make love to my husband and then report back to you with how things went before you'll release me? Did I get that right?" I was sure he hadn't had both oars in the water. I felt like I was twelve and reporting to the principal's office. What was that all about?

"Yep, you got it right, Carroll. Now, can you tell me why this is important?" He asked, noticing the blank expression on my face.

"No, for God's sake. I cannot imagine why?" I answered, my face filled with confusion.

"Art?" How about you? Can you tell me why?" he asked.

"Honestly, I cannot." Art answered, equally confused.

"It's quite simple. You have been through a very traumatic time in your life, everything is still new and there is a measure of reluctance on your part to fully accept that you won't come apart if you're touched. You both are part of this life-altering experience and I don't want it to be your excuse, Carroll, for building a wall around you. I've been doing this a very long time and believe me when I tell you it's most important to not only have a strong and healthy marriage, but you need to have a healthy sex life as well. Too many marriages fall apart because the patient is afraid. Or their spouse is afraid. I've seen it happen time and time again. That's why it's important for you to do as I'm suggesting. I don't want to see it happen to you.

"There'll be times during lovemaking when you'll have a leak or your bag may come off. All of this is normal. You aren't the first person to have an ileostomy and you won't be the last.

This is my reason for having my patients spend a night together before being released. And if it takes more than a night, so be it. It's for the emotional welfare of both of you. Are we in agreement?"

"I guess we don't have much choice." I said. "Do we?"

"No you don't. It's for your own good that I'm doing this. Someday you'll understand.

But Carroll, tell me, what's really bothering you? I noticed it when I first mentioned spending the night as husband and wife. An immediate shield went up and you quickly attempted to conceal your fears and anxiety. Isn't this right?"

A terrifying cloud hovered above me. He hit the nail on the head and there would be no trying to fool this man. He knew me better than I knew myself, it seemed. I had to answer him.

"I'm afraid. I'm really, really terrified," I said, through a blur of tears. A trace of shame written on my face. Crying as if sorrow would somehow shut out the shame.

"Terrified of what?" he asked in a kind and gentle manner.

"That's just it. I really don't know! I think maybe it's the pain I'll experience as I move about. Or . . . or . . . I'm afraid everything will come apart. It'll all fall off. I don't know how I'm supposed to feel. To react. How could I possibly know these answers?" Tears came to my eyes, magnifying and distorting the scene into a great hazy blur.

"God, I'm such a baby. How in hell can I go on when I don't know what to do? I don't know how to feel. I don't have any answers and once I leave here who do I talk to if I need help. If I have questions. I'll be like a ship without a rudder floating aimlessly through a black cold sea."

Racked with sobs, Art took me in his arms and just held me. And I held on for dear life, afraid to let go.

"Listen to me, Carroll, and please listen well. I'm going to tell you something that has the greatest potential of all to insure your success at the way you handle your disease. Because it's not going away. You'll have Crohn's disease forever. It's not a curable disease. Your ileostomy is also not going away. That, too, you will have forever. But there is something you and only you can do to insure a successful, happy, and fulfilled life."

He waited until I turned and looked at him. It was important that he look into my eyes for me to really understand what he was about to tell me.

As I wiped the tears from my eyes and the sniffles from my nose, I finally asked the most important question of my life. "What, pray tell, could you possibly say that I haven't already heard? Nothing will change how I feel about this disgusting thing I have to look at and take care of the rest of my life. Huh? What am I saying? Further more, what am I thinking? How could you possibly know?" I implied with a great deal of defiance. "You don't have an ileostomy. Only those, like me, could even begin to understand what I'm going through," I said raising my voice as I stood pacing the office, ranting and raving.

"Carroll! Sit. Down." Art said, as a flash of embarrassment at my outburst slid across his face.

"No, Art. Let her talk. She needs to do this," my doctor said, reclining in his chair.

I rolled with such intense verbal blows, my tears were even afraid to peek out of my eyes.

"If you feel you have to throw something, throw it. But please, not at me or at Art. And for God's sake and mine, please don't throw that figurine." He pointed at a beautiful bronze bust. "My wife bought it for me for our anniversary and she would be royally pissed. The last thing I need is a pissed-off wife." He raised his eyebrows attempting to stifle a smile.

I abruptly stopped my frantic, ridiculous ranting, gesturing, and pacing. I stood there dead still wondering what in hell I was doing. I wasn't even quite sure what I'd said. But I had a pretty good idea as I turned and looked at Art, that it probably wasn't my finest moment.

Loosing my rigidity, I turned slowly and shamefully slithered into my chair. I was mortified at my loss of control and too mortified to even speak. The quiet in that room was stifling. Not a word was spoken. I waited, hoping someone would break the silence. I would have a very long wait. I sat shredding my tissues in my hands, too embarrassed to lift my head and face the music. Gradually, with a gesture of resignation, I raised my hands and my eyes in supplication, beseeching forgiveness.

With a voice scarcely audible, I said, "So sorry about all that. I think I'm ready to hear what you were trying to tell me before I went ballistic on both of you. And for the record, I would never have thrown anything. I'm not a thrower. I'm a yeller, I guess."

Both men laughed and I released a very grateful sigh of relief.

Chapter 17

The message my doctor imparted that day was one which I've carried with me everyday of my life. They were the most powerful nine words I'd ever heard. And to him I shall be eternally grateful.

He very simply said, "It can control you, or you can control it." Nine powerful and formidable words! With those words, I began to realize that the onus was now on my tiny shoulders. It was up to me and me alone to control my life. My disease. I don't profess to imply that it was all roses and sunshine. I'd be lying if I did that. And I will not lie to you. You deserve more.

Throughout the past forty-plus years of having to deal with all sorts of issues regarding either my Crohn's or my ileostomy, has proven a wealth of information. I'm my own lab study, my own lab specimen. Each episode, either physical or mental regarding the alteration of my journey, I would be brought back by a mere prick of a thorn reminding me that as beautiful as a rose is, you had to be prepared to be pricked by one of her thorns.

I can assure you that as you traverse down your own slippery slopes of life, you'll have many bumps, many falls, and many detours along the way. I am hopeful that you too will remember for the rest of your life, those nine powerful words: *It Can Control You or You Can Control It.*

Giving up or giving in, my friends, is never an option. But continuing on, *is*. It's your only option. Living your life to its fullest. Thanking God on a daily basis for allowing you to spend another day on this earth. To share your love, your beliefs, and yes, your good fortune of just being alive with your family and friends.

I'm here to tell you that I've been up and I've been down because of my Crohn's or my ileostomy. But no matter how down I get, I seem to find the strength to claw my way back up. Somehow those all-important nine words come creeping from a safe place in my mind, in my heart, and remind me that life is too precious to give up. That I'm too special to quit.

Oh, you'll continue to question, *why me?* Maybe you'll never have your whys answered. But, then again if you're not willing to move ahead with your life, you'll never know.

It's not what we look at that matters, but, what we see. When diverse perceptions struggle against one another, the truth somehow, rather sadly, has a way of being set adrift and a most unfortunate thing happens; our worst monsters find a way of slipping out.

Stop questioning and start believing and you'll keep your monsters at bay.

"Oh, I nearly forgot to tell you something very important. Yes, we did spend our night together as husband and wife in Art's hotel room, and believe it or not, everything worked just as it should have. And everything stayed in place just as my doctor said it would. He was a very wise man. It should be mandatory that doctors insist their patients spend a night alone with their spouse or significant other.

"I will forever be eternally grateful for finally understanding precisely what he was so patiently attempting to tell me that final day of my hospitalization. Just that one small directive from a very caring doctor, was enormously rewarding, reassuring, and life-altering.

Chapter 18

It was now May and I was finally home with my children, my husband, and my Heidi. That was the best medicine I could have ever wished for. My recovery was slow, but it grew steadier month to month. Walking became much easier. Bathing and changing my appliance were becoming less rigorous. I was gradually learning to break those chains that seemed to be holding me captive in my own home.

My hair, as I mentioned earlier in my story, was very thick and long, hanging just below my shoulders. But something strange was beginning to happen to it. Something I was not prepared for. What I was not told at the hospital, or if I was I certainly hadn't remembered, was as I began my regimen of tapering off the steroids my hair would begin to fall out.

It scared me to death one morning when I was washing my hair and began seeing it on the shower floor. At first, it was only small amounts. That was a little disheartening, to say the least. But the day I saw it in clumps, literally bunches of black hair on the shower floor, I couldn't begin to fathom what was happening to me. As I gently tugged on my hair, I found myself holding a long clump in my hand and I began to cry. Thank God Art was at home. He heard me calling him and came into the bathroom and discovered what looked like a dead animal on my shower floor.

"What in hell happened?" he asked.

Through a deluge of tears and eyes wide with fear, I managed to say, "My hair is falling out. I'm going bald. What else could possibly happen to me that hasn't already happened? Why is God doing this to me? Haven't I been through enough horror in my life? Now, I'm going bald." My hand flew to my mouth in an effort to somehow divert the tears and fear I was now experiencing.

"Okay. First of all, the doctors said you might lose your hair. They didn't know how much, however. And, secondly, hair grows back. Until that time, you can wear a wig. They make some pretty nice ones nowadays. No one will be the wiser. But before we do that, I'm going to call your beauty shop and see if he'll get you in earlier than everyone else so he can cut your hair really short and in the privacy of his shop. No one will see you. You can be in and out before his other clientele arrive. I'll even go with you if you like? How does that sound?"

"Good. Really good. I'll just wear scarves until I can get in to see him. Will you call him now for me? I'd really appreciate it."

"Will do. Honey, please don't worry. It'll be fine. Now, where do I find his number?"

"In my desk, in the red phone book, under *The Gazebo*," I answered, as I began rinsing the shampoo from my hair. I suddenly smiled at what the hair on the floor must have looked like to Art. It certainly caught his full attention.

"Okay Carroll, it's now time to wipe the incident of this morning from your mind." I said, becoming fascinated by my own attitude. "Just a few weeks ago I would have crumbled into a pile on the bathroom floor. Good for me. I'm powerful, I'm alive, and I'll get through this thing one day, one week, one month, and one year at a time. Little baby steps is all it takes, Carroll. And with your size ten shoe, your little baby steps will bring you a lot closer and a lot more quickly to winning the game than someone with only a size six."

I started laughing while I began to realize that my interior sun shone more brightly now than it did yesterday. It was a delicious self-approval. There were no more shadows of sadness to be seen. With an over-powering, irresistible vitality, I was ready to take on the world, either with or without hair.

CHAPTER 19

During my first year at home and adjusting to my ileostomy, I discovered that all ostomies are not created equal. In other words, on several occasions while out to dinner with Art and friends, I had some mishaps.

One in particular bears telling. It was a Christmas formal and my ileostomy decided to make its presence known to all. As it turned out, I was the only one who realized what was happening. I discovered my leak when I went to the ladies room. Oh boy, did I have a situation. It was my first problem like this . . . *ever*. I guess I need to clarify that statement. It was the first time I had a leak in public.

My girlfriend made a beeline to tell Art that we had to go home immediately. I had a medical repair to make.

I will now reveal one of life's greatest mysteries asked by every man every where. "Why do women always go to the ladies room in pairs?" Now you have your answer. It's in case one of us has an emergency of any kind.

"I was so nervous and was certain that we wouldn't make it home in time without ruining my ball gown. But, somehow we managed. Maybe it was all the toilet tissue I'd stuffed into my pantyhose to stop the ebb and flow of my stoma which really saved the day. That and a lot of praying didn't hurt, either.

"To this day, I still break out into laughter thinking what must have been running through the mind of our babysitter when we arrived home after only two hours and headed straight back to our bedroom. There we spent about an hour or so, while Art helped me out of my gown, out of my pantyhose, helped me change my appliance, and then helped me back into fresh pantyhose, and back into my gown. He waited patiently until I adjusted and readjusted everything that ladies had to adjust and readjust. We left our bedroom, telling the babysitter goodnight for the second time, got back in the car and continued to the ball. I'm sure she had a great story to tell her friends or her mother.

"Art and I still laugh about that evening. I hope that if you find yourself in a situation like mine, you'll take time to laugh about it afterward. It wasn't as bad as I thought. I did what had to be done and continued on with the rest of my evening. Sipping champagne and tripping the light fantastic.

"Trust me, you'll run into situations similar to mine. That one was an easy one to take care of. I had another that wasn't as simple. I was in United Airlines' Red Carpet Club at O'Hare Airport in Chicago when I discovered I had a leak. I was alone and had no option except to try and repair it by myself.

"I first went back out to the clubroom, picked up my tote, took it and myself back to the restroom. I used the wheelchair stall in the bathroom, sat on the commode and changed my appliance as best I could, under the circumstances I was dealing with. I finished, went back out, sat down, and read my book until they called my flight. I had no problems whatsoever on the plane and when I got to where I was going, I changed it again using the prescribed method. Just to be on the safe side. Actually, it was for my own peace of mind.

Nothing more.

Why, you may be asking yourself, is she telling me these tales of horror? Well, I only hope you don't find yourself in the same predicaments as I was in; but, if you do, you'll know that you can do whatever it takes to remedy the problem.

I can just about guarantee that as long as you have an ileostomy, you'll one day find yourself face to face with that elephant in the room. But, I also can guarantee, that you'll know what to do if you are prepared ahead of time. Maybe my little tales of woe will lead you in the direction of self-preparation. Once is all it took for me to wake me up to the fact that I should carry a small selection of supplies with me. Especially, if I'm going to be far away from home. And by far away, I mean over an hour. This way you'll be ready to tackle whatever pops up.

And things always have a way of popping up at the most inopportune times. As they say, "Chance favors the prepared mind."

Having an ostomy of any kind and/or Crohn's disease, will force you to live differently than you perhaps have been living. It will teach you to always live life on your own hook. Be your own person. And while living your life, learn to live it to the fullest. Be the best *you,* you can be. The best brother, the best sister, the best mother, the best father, the best son, the best daughter, the best husband, or the best wife. It's a gift that is worth having, but, more importantly, it's a gift worth sharing.

Always approach your life with a sense of humor. There's nothing you can do to change what has happened, but there's a lot you can do to change the outcome of your life. Your future . . . You're alive, for God's sake. Embrace it. So what if you're inconvenienced a little or a lot?

You. Are. Alive. Don't ever forget that!

Chapter 20

It's been more than forty years of battling pain, hospitalization, trips to the E.R. because of blockages, and the list goes on. Crohn's Disease is a tough disease. It's also one no one wants to talk about; hence, forcing most to suffer in silence, unwilling to share our malady. I'm not going to tell you that any disease is glamorous, but most diseases are at least discussed at forums, on talk shows, and various other venues.

Take it from me, one who knows firsthand; no one wants to talk about *poop*. Yep, that's what I said. Poop!

There has always been this strange stigma attached to our bodily functions. It's led seemingly to the brunt of millions of jokes and stories. Yet, we all have to carry them out in one form or another. Mine, like many others, means eliminating into a pouch attached to my tummy, and then emptying the contents into the commode; thus, affording me the luxury of **living.** Of simply being alive. Were it not for that pouch, I would not be here right now explaining how you can cope or how you can help others to cope with their disease.

Others' elimination process is to empty into the toilet that which must be taken care of.

Albeit, the same process, different vessels. See we're not so different after all. Are we?

The one thing I have going for me that you don't, however, is I go big potty when it's convenient for me. When I decide I want to empty my pouch.

Now, *you,* on the other hand, are a different kettle of fish. You have no voice in the matter as to when you go. When you have to go . . . *You have to go.*

So you see, having an ileostomy has a *few* redeeming qualities. Don't get me wrong. I would much prefer your method of elimination to mine, any day. But since I don't have that luxury, I elect to see the positive side of a negative situation. You know, like looking at the glass as being half full instead of half empty.

If I can carry on living a pretty darn good life, it is possible for you to do the same. But, before you can, you must decide it's what you want to do more than anything else. Because being alive is so much more rewarding than the alternative. That alternative, my friends, is unacceptable. Death is never an option when you can do something about it. Even on your worst days, death is a poor substitute for living. But, that's just my opinion.

If you are worried about traveling, please don't. I have traveled all over the world on planes, trains, buses, and ships, and have done it feeling great and at times not so great. I've hiked the wilds of Alaska, snorkeled the blue waters of the Caribbean, went fly fishing in Yellowstone, and explored the amazing Glacier National Park. I've walked the great White Cliffs of Dover, strolled the beautiful paths and lanes of the British Isles. I've shopped the stores of Hong Kong and Tokyo, skied some the most majestic mountains in the world, in both Europe and the USA and took an archeological tour of the Coliseum in Rome. I even had the distinct pleasure of holding a koala bear in my arms in Australia. I've spent a month in Germany with my girlfriend visiting her family in Bavaria. I've done things alone and I've done things with my husband and family. You see, I was actually doing things I thought I'd *never* be able to do again because of my ileostomy.

It was especially interesting when Art and I were in Japan, having coffee in a small café. I had to make a trip to the restroom. I knew which one to use as I'd studied my Japanese tapes on the long flight over. However, when I entered I got a real surprise. I thought I was in the men's room. So I backed out, looked again at the door, reassuring myself that I hadn't made a mistake.

I re-entered, checked the three stalls that were there. They were all the same. Each was equipped with a large hole in the floor. There was no way I was going to attempt that. You'd have had to have been a gymnast to be able to squat that low and still remain standing. Americans are not built to squat. Especially not this American. I whistled on out of there and told Art that we would have to go back to the hotel for me to be able to take care of my business.

You may find yourself in the same predicament one day. I guarantee you'll also find a way out of it, just as I did. And, in the process, be able to laugh at yourself.

But it was the winter of 1974 that I decided to face the biggest challenge of my life. I decided that simply because I had an ileostomy it should not curtail me from doing what I loved to do; and, that was snow ski.

Art made all the arrangements and off we went to Engelberg, Switzerland, with both children and all our ski gear in tow and began a two week skiing adventure of a lifetime. We'd skied Austria, Germany and the United States before, but this was the first with our children abroad.

While the kids and I went to ski school for a few days to brush up on our skiing, Art went off skiing with friends he'd met. He'd joined us each afternoon after our school was over and we skied as a family the rest of the day. I was in ski school for two days and the kids were in ski school for five, as their goal was to learn to ski the harder courses with their instructors so they could earn special medals and certificates. We looked on with great pride as their instructors presented their medals and certificates at an awards ceremony. If you're a parent, then you know how thrilling it is for kids to achieve their goals.

It wasn't long before they were skiing the Titlis Glacier with Art and me. It was a real achievement for the kids and for me. If you've ever skied the Swiss Alps, then you are aware of the mighty Titlis Glacier and how challenging it really is. You're skiing from the top of the glacier on pure ice, from 10,623 feet. I figured if I could master that with my ileostomy, then there should be little else I would be unable to accomplish in life.

Now you can see why I chose this particular cover for my book. *I was the lone skier.*

I knew if I could do this, then anyone out there who wished to tackle their challenge, no matter what it was or where it was, would be able to do just that. I'm not going to tell you that I wasn't afraid, because I was. Actually, terrified might be a better description.

"Are you certain you want to do this?" Art asked as we all stood on the platform staring down at nothing but ice. "There's still time to turn around and ride the cable car back down. You've done a hell of a job already. You really don't have to do this, you know. Plus, the fog's rolling in. We've got to leave now or we'll never find our way down the mountain."

"No. I can do this. Actually, Art, I *have* to do this. It's for me. It's my challenge and I intend to see it through. So, let's go." I said, cranking up my courage, wondering if I'd bitten off more than I could chew. I knew if I didn't, I'd always have that question hanging over my head. *Could I have done it and why did I refuse to try.* I placed my fears in my pocket of my ski parka and headed down the ice chute with my family to face my fears head on. It was the most exhilarating feeling of my life. One I'll forever remember.

So my friends, I challenge you to face your fears, big or small, and go for it. It makes no difference what it is as long as you try. Maybe skiing isn't your thing, but perhaps your family would love to attempt it. Go along and enjoy all the things the area has to offer and join them at the top of the mountain for lunch, enjoy learning about their day, and when they leave to continue skiing, you head back down to town on the cable car and do some shopping, enjoy the village and the townspeople. Visit the quaint café's for coffee and a pastry. Go to the small chocolate shops and select some handmade incredible chocolates and surprise your family with these delectable delights when they arrive back from their day of skiing. They'll love you for it.

I don't ski anymore and that's because of my coordination problems stemming from my 2002 debacle. It would not be advisable for me to attempt even a bunny slope. However, I still travel with my family and do exactly what I'd encouraged you to do in the above paragraphs. I'll wander around the town of Steamboat Springs, Colorado, meet and talk with all the shop owners and have coffee and a pastry in a small café or coffee shop. I sometimes meet my family on the mountain for lunch or may elect to lunch alone. But I'm still an integral part of their lives.

I hope you're beginning to realize that you can travel with ease and enjoy the same places that your family may wish to. You don't have to travel the world to know you can travel. That was not my intention when I told you this story. I simply wanted you to know that you can enjoy life with your family and friends even if you're not interested in doing the same things as they are. It's amazing how you seem to learn to appreciate the simple things you were certain you would *never* want to do. Enjoy their company. Be a part of their lives. Take a walk or a drive in the country. Rent a movie and make it a fun family night. Pack a picnic lunch and enjoy the sunset no matter where in the world it's setting, even if it's in your own backyard. Please don't forget to enjoy your life and *never* forget to share it with your family. It's so very important to do those little things. If you remember to take care of the little things, the big ones will take care of themselves. That's why we have medications and doctors who understand what we're dealing with. Yes, you might have to make some allowances to what you wear, at times. Or what you eat. Some days you can eat an elephant and have no repercussions and other days, a glass of milk will send you to the moon and back. But over time, you learn to understand and respect your body and what it is or is not telling you.

You'll make mistakes. We all make mistakes. Even after forty plus years, I still make mistakes. I know there are things I should probably *never* eat and yet, I still do. Sometimes I get away with it, and other times, not so much. It's those times when I've eaten the proverbial no-no, *popcorn* in my case, that I've had horrible intestinal cramping. I mean pain like a woman has during childbirth and on several occasions, much worse, if that's even possible. It's times like those that I find myself in the Emergency Room having a tube shoved down my nose and into my stomach to bypass the blockage. Not fun at all. Don't you think I would have learned my lesson? Well, for a little while, yes; I was a good girl and ate only what I should be eating and no unwelcomed goodies.

The times you think you have the world by the tail, is exactly the time you should prepare yourself to have that tail whip around and knock you on your . . . backside.

Please don't forget that you are only in remission. You are *not* cured. You'll never be cured. I don't want you to go around as though you have the sword of Domocles hanging over your head just waiting for the moment to fall upon you. Not at all. Quite the contrary. I only want you to keep in the back of your mind, that remission means simply the lessening of your symptoms. They are always going to be there. The longer you do what you should be doing, food wise, the longer you'll be in remission.

There are other factors besides diet, of course, but that seems to be the biggest contributor. So be astute when it comes to what you consume. You'll screw up. Like I said before, I still screw up and I should certainly know better. Just don't allow yourself to fall prey to apathy. You can sit and watch your life go by or you can join the parade and enjoy every moment. Learn from the stressful parts and enjoy the journey. No matter how hard you try, none of us are getting out of our life alive. It's important not to define yourself by what you do, but by who you are. There is a quotation I'm particularly fond of.

"There is a giant asleep within every man. When the giant awakes, miracles happen."

Frederick Faust (1892 – 1944)

I'm of the opinion that people will tell you who they are if you just learn to listen. I also think we write our own stories, and each time we think we know the ending, we come to the realization that we *don't*.

Maybe it's time for you to write your own story. Not necessarily putting it on paper, although that certainly wouldn't hurt. Keeping a journal is a good thing. If you don't want to write it on paper then write it in your head on a daily basis. Do something positive. If you are suffering, reach out and ask for help. And if you can, join a local Crohn's/Colitis, Ostomy or IBD Support Group. Your hospital or doctor can probably help you find one. Or perhaps the ostomy nurse where you purchase your supplies.

And most importantly, join the Crohn's and Colitis Foundation of America. They have a wealth of information at your disposal. Use it. Use them. That's what they're there for. I know, I use their information all the time either for myself or to help others.

THE MIDDLE – Sarasota, Florida 2002

CHAPTER 21

In the winter of 2002, I found myself battling the remission thing all over again. The steroids that usually worked were having absolutely no affect. Steroids are a good thing when you are so ill, but they do irreparable damage to your body. And having been on them for long periods of my life, more than forty years off and on, they certainly had taken their toll on me.

My symptoms had come back to haunt me. I was hospitalized on Tuesday, March 5, for some surgery to remove what they thought was either adhesions or more diseased bowel. But they couldn't be certain until they had the small intestine on the table and saw firsthand for themselves.

However, my surgery had to be postponed until March 7, because of very low blood pressure. The anesthesiologist didn't want to take a chance on someone with such low blood pressure. So they rolled me back to my room. Yep, I found myself coming and going at the same time. I had to wait until my blood pressure was stabile enough to try surgery again.

Swirled in confusion until finally at 5:30 pm on March 7, I was wheeled into the operating room where they did some minor repairs, sutured me up, and sent me briefly to recovery.

If I had lived in some third world country, perhaps that would have been acceptable. But I wasn't in a third-world country; I was in Sarasota, a large city thought to have some pretty talented surgeons and some pretty good hospitals.

That little move would prove to be the beginning of the end of my life.

While I was being moved to recovery, my surgeon came out to talk to my family reassuring them that although he'd seen something on my small bowel that appeared it could be a problem, he'd made a judgment call and decided to bypass the problem.

After knowing what he knew, it should have been imperative to him that my time in recovery would be long enough for the nurses to have detected what was about to happen. No one should be sent to their room until their recovery is more than stable. No doctor should ever be allowed to make that mistake. My family questioned his decision, but was assured I was in good hands. He also suggested that after Art was able to see me in recovery, he go home until the next morning. Most likely with the meds he prescribed, I would sleep through the night.

Big Mistake. *Huge mistake!* We were about to learn just how bad his decision was.

Thinking I was probably doing okay, I drifted in and out of consciousness which was a normal symptom of someone who's just been through surgery. My vitals appeared normal and I seemed to be doing pretty well. My family was assured that I would be fine. I was resting comfortably, so they returned home to get a good night's sleep. They had been up early and were at the hospital all day long awaiting my surgery. It had been a really long day for them.

Alone in my private room in the early hours of March 8, I began feeling odd. I was experiencing some rather intense pain. Through years of dealing with my Crohn's and my ileostomy, I'd become a pretty good judge of my body when it told me something was not right. Well, it was sure telling me now. My pain continued to grow in intensity and each time I rang my call button, the nurse said to simply press my pain medication button to increase my morphine. Which I did, continued to do, but to no avail. Nothing was working. In fact, I was even beginning to question if the pain pump was actually functional. It sure didn't seem to be doing its job.

For hours I suffered with increasingly intense pain, the kind of pain that makes you cry out loud to God to make it stop. Even the on-duty doctor didn't seem to find it necessary to come and examine me; he simply instructed the nurse to increase my pain meds.

I heard the nurse enter my room and quietly approach my bed. "Carroll, how's the pain?"

"Worse than it was the last time you asked me." I answered. Eyes wide with fear. With doubt.

"The doctor said I could increase your morphine."

"Please. You've got to help me. Something is very wrong." I cried. My eyes filled with the unnerving, hopeless horror a canary must feel just before the cat makes her move.

"Why is everyone refusing to listen to me? I know what I'm talking about. This pain isn't normal. Please help me. Please, oh please, help me." I said as the nurse made the adjustment on my morphine pump.

"That should help. Try and relax and get some rest." The nurse said, and left the room.

I had an overwhelming premonition of disaster. And there wasn't a damn thing I could do about it.

I could feel my consciousness begin to diffuse. My eyes began to take on the slightly unfocused glare typical of fever while terror engulfed me. I hung on 'til morning terrified to go to sleep for fear of never waking up. The pain was indescribable.

My gastroenterologist, Dr. Quinn, arrived earlier than usual that morning. I would later find out that something told him to get to the hospital in a hurry. Or was it someone? A higher power? I think I already knew the answer to that.

He walked into my room, took one look at me, and issued a "CODE RED." He immediately notified my surgeon, who was still at home. He notified the operating room informing I was in distress, to prepare for my immediate arrival and my surgeon was on his way.

"Hang in there Carroll. Help is on its way."

"Please. Help. Me. Something. Wrong." Those were the last words I remember uttering.

"Stay with me, Carroll. Come on, I know you can do it. Just a little while longer." Dr. Quinn needed only a look to tell there was a problem which needed to be taken care of . . . **now!**

Fighting for my life, I struggled as long as possible to stay conscious, all the while feeling an overwhelming terror place its icy finger in my heart and wrapped its cold tentacles around it, squeezing until I could feel no more. I had lost consciousness momentarily. As I was being coded and rushed out of my room, I heard Dr. Quinn making one more call.

"Mr. deCarle, it's Dr. Quinn. You need to get here as quickly as possible. And you'll need to notify your family." He spoke with a voice filled with concern. His undertone of meaning was unmistakable.

Caught completely off guard, Art didn't know what to say. And then in a somewhat strangled voice, he asked, "What happened?" In a voice strained with pain, he asked, "What in hell happened? She was fine last night when we left."

"They're rushing her to surgery. And I don't know what her chances are. When I saw her, she didn't look good at all. Her pain was out of control. Her body was racked with fever. I have a theory that the intestine ruptured and her body's been invaded by sepsis. She appears to be in septic shock. Art, I'm afraid to say this, but she may not last the day."

"Shit!! Art said, confused and frightened.

"We'll talk when you get here. Just have me paged. But make those calls now. Your family needs to know and they need to be here."

"I'll be there shortly. Thanks." Frantically, he somehow managed to get dressed while making calls, was quickly out the door, jumped in the car and and on his way.

CHAPTER 22

Art had Dr. Quinn paged and was told to go to the waiting room on the fourth floor where he'd be met. When Art got off the elevator, Dr. Quinn was waiting for him and escorted him to an empty office.

"What happened?" Art asked, out of breath and desperate for answers.

"When I entered her room early this morning, I knew immediately she was in trouble. Her pleas for help were gut wrenching. Just the way she looked at me and said, 'I prayed you'd come. Help me. Please. No one helped me. No one listened. Pain. So. Bad!'"

As if momentarily lost in a haze of grief, Dr. Quinn quickly recovered, pulled himself back, looked at Art with sadness in his eyes, and began. "Before she finished talking, I called code red. Which means . . ."

"I know what it means." Art said, interrupting.

"Of course."

"Where is she now?" Art asked, his mind too clouded, too unsure.

"She's still in surgery. Her heart stopped and they had to use the paddles. Her lungs collapsed. Her kidney's failed. All organs shut down."

"Dear Jesus, why?"

"The pain she was complaining about was indeed real. Her intestine had ruptured and sepsis began running rampant through her body for at least twelve hours, I'm guessing."

"What the hell is sepsis?" Art asked, raking his hands through his hair as he seemed to sink lower and lower into the chair.

"It's a complex illness involving both infection and inflammation. Normally, the body's response to an infection is targeted at the site of the infection. With sepsis, the body's response instead of being localized at the site causes symptoms to occur throughout the body. Carroll showed many of the signs of the systemic response when I first saw her.

She had a fever, severe pain, a distended belly, her heart was beating faster than normal and her breathing was labored. All of these things caused the infection to spin out of control upsetting her body's state of balance. And we already know her organs were compromised. They all shut down.

"For Carroll, with her Crohn's and her already compromised immune system, she's very much at risk. Severe sepsis is a very serious, life-threatening condition. Organs may not receive enough oxygen and they may fail or shut down as hers did. When organs shut down, important functions of the body cannot occur. The more organs that shut down, the greater the risk of death.

"Shit! Will she be alright? Tell me she'll be alright. Please." Art felt the weight of his world pushing down upon his shoulders like a ten ton boulder.

"I wish I could. But, please let me finish what I was explaining. Patients who survive severe sepsis are likely to stay in CCU until their organs begin working properly. The condition of the patient after the episode varies depending on several factors, such as the patient's health before the episode and how severe their disease was. In some cases the areas most affected could be physical activity, communication, and energy level."

"What in hell are you saying? She might not be able to walk or talk?"

"I just don't know. Long-term effects may include organ damage. That could be permanent or temporary, but for now we simply don't know. Despite these challenges, many people who survive can make a full recovery and return to their daily activities.

"For now, we'll let the surgeons do what they must to save her life and get things stabilized, and then we'll just wait. That will be the hardest. The waiting."

"I hope to hell the surgeons do a better job this time. I certainly don't put much faith in their ability." Art said, shaking his head. "Shit!"

"With what happened, I don't think you have to worry. They have several surgeons with her this time around. I think they'll be okay and so will Carroll. Have you called your family?"

"Yes. My son and daughter-in-law and our friends are on their way."

"What about your daughter?"

"She's in Tennessee and she's making arrangements to be on the first flight out."

"When your family and friends arrive, they'll be brought here. If you like, you're welcome to remain here or I've made arrangements for you to use a private waiting room. You might be more comfortable there. It's equipped with comfortable couches and chairs. It has a television and a coffee machine."

"That sounds fine. When will we know something about Carroll?"

"As soon as I know, you'll know. I promise you. In the meantime, I'll be happy to stay with you until your family arrives. If you would like?"

"I'd like that." Art said, bereft of all understanding. He walked toward the window, stood there and gazed out at nothingness. Stunned and grief-stricken, fighting with all his might to keep his overwhelming sadness at bay; but, secretly wishing the ground would just swallow him up.

"Why did this happen?" he asked, more to himself than anyone else. And then the final, icy comprehension of what he feared, spread through him like a raging river. His strong demeanor slipped quietly away and the tears he'd been unwilling to shed, poured forth like a waterfall flowing over his cheeks, landing silently on the window sill. "Dear God, why?" he cried.

Leaving him to his privacy, Dr. Quinn slipped quietly outside the door where he waited in silence asking himself the same question. *Why?*

Allowing Art sufficient time to gather himself, he knocked softly on the door.

"Come in." Art replied.

"Can I get you anything?"

"Some water would be great. Thanks."

Dr. Quinn called the nurses station requesting a carafe of water and glasses.

"It'll be here shortly. Art, I want you to know something. Carroll must have a will of steel because she hung onto life, refusing to give up on the fact that help would come. The sheer number of hours she was in such severe pain, and still didn't give up, blows my mind. I cannot begin to explain just how bad her pain must have been. It would have put down a rhino; yet she hung in there. She's one mentally tough lady. If anyone can beat her odds, she can. I think she has a guardian angel riding on her shoulder."

"Thanks, doc. I appreciate that. I think a lot of prayers are in order as well. She's doing her job. Now, we need to do ours." Art said, with a voice lacking confidence.

Just then there was a knock at the door and the nurse entered with a carafe of ice water and four glasses. Behind her, his son, Mac, and his wife, Jennifer, arrived.

"I'll leave you with your family and I'll have a nurse show you to your waiting room, if you'd like."

"Thank you."

"You bet. The operating room has my pager. They'll let me know when surgery is over. I'll call and come by to let you know what happened and what to expect."

Art shook his head, while Jennifer guided him to a seat.

Mac walked the doctor through the doorway, closing the door behind him. "Is there anything you need to tell me that you haven't told my dad?" Mac asked.

"No. I was brutally honest with your dad. It wasn't a time to sugar-coat things. He'll tell you precisely what I told him. He promised me he'd do just that."

"Thanks, Doctor Quinn for everything, especially for staying with my dad until we were able to get here. It means a great deal to our family."

"It was the least I could do, Mac. Now you go on back in there with him. I'll keep you updated."

They shook hands, each going his separate way. A nurse escorted everyone to a waiting room and the long wait began.

CHAPTER 23

M y family and friends spent many collective hours in the hospital chapel. Was time to be their enemy or their friend? Each afraid to give in to what might be, how their lives could suddenly change forever. Would they be granted one more chance to say all the things they hadn't, but wished they had? Just one more chance to laugh, to cry, to be forgiven. Would they ever get that chance?

The next hours and days would tell. Time was the one commodity they could not hoard. But now, every second seemed like hours and each person had fallen into an isolated cubicle of time.

Art kept watching the clock on the wall willing the hands of time to move faster. It had taken only a few ticks of time to send his world as he'd known it, spiraling into a vortex of an unknown. And right about now, he wanted to rip the damn clock off the wall. But he was smart enough to realize that no matter what damage he was able to inflict upon the clock, it would make not one iota of difference. Time would still continue to tick by, one second, one minute, one lonely hour, at a time. The clock stared back as if mocking him.

If only he could turn back the hands of time. "If only . . ." he cried in an inaudible voice. In an agony of impatience, he blurted out, "Shit!"

Everyone turned, not knowing what or if they should say or do anything. So they said and did nothing, knowing his outburst needed no response. Time simply dragged on as the minutes stubbornly refused to move.

Each time the door open everyone jumped, not really prepared to hear what they might be forced to hear.

Around 1P.M., Dr. Quinn returned with some news. When he entered there were six sets of eyes facing him. No one willing to ask the question, "How is she?"

"I want to tell you, she made it through surgery. But, she's on life support and is in the critical care unit where she'll be monitored twenty four hours a day. They're flushing the sepsis from her body which will take time. She had to be given blood during her surgery. Quite frankly, she's a marvel. The amount of sepsis raging through her body was unbelievable. Why in hell she's still with us is a miracle."

Everyone hugged one another and began to cry.

"When can I see her?" Art asked.

"It'll be awhile. Right now we're getting her all set up in CCU and the meds that are being used to flush the sepsis out of her body have plumped her up. Don't be alarmed when you see her. It's only temporary."

"Thanks, Doctor."

"You're very welcome. But I must warn you, she's not out of the woods yet. The next several days are critical ones. If she gets through that, she's one step closer to recovering. Okay?"

"Okay."

"I'll send a nurse to get you after she's settled. We intend to keep her sedated for now. She's in a lot of pain and she won't know you're there, but you need to see her for yourself. It'll do you good.

"I've got to run. I've got some patients to see, but I'll check in on you later. If you need anything, please have the nurse page me."

Everyone thanked him and before he left, he said, "I suggest you all get some rest and some food. It's going to be a long few days."

Earlier that day, Courtney had advised Art that her flight would arrive in Tampa from Memphis at four P.M. Art told her that Uncle Pete and Auntie Barb would be picking her and the boys up.

Courtney had been so devastated by the news from Art about her mother that she could scarcely function enough to call her friends to come and help her pack.

One friend picked up Alex from school, while the others helped Courtney pack for herself, Alex, and Cameron.

The girls drove them to the airport and waited til their plane took off.

Courtney and her boys were on their way. The plane soared skyward like a homesick angel carrying precious cargo toward the foggy grayness of the unknown.

Barb and Pete were there to pick them up at the Tampa Airport, drove them home to drop off their luggage, and then onto the hospital.

Barb and Pete kept the little ones occupied, after accompanying Courtney to the waiting room and her family.

Courtney opened the door terrified at what she might hear. When she spied Art, she flew into her Dad's arms and cried holding on for dear life.

"It's okay, Honey." Art held her and let her cry until she was all cried out.

"Oh, daddy, how's she doing? I don't understand any of this. She was fine last night." She said with a heart too heavy for anyone to have to bear.

"Let's sit down over here and I'll explain everything that I know. She's alive and in CCU, but what happened to her is unbelievable." Art began explaining what had happened from this morning until now. He prepared her as best he could for when she stepped into her mother's room.

Apparently I didn't look quite like myself.

Pete and Barb took the boys to the cafeteria to get them something to eat as well as to try and take their minds off of their Nana.

Courtney walked into the room, took one look at the person lying in bed with tubes, machines, and wires everywhere, turned around, made a hasty retreat, and approached the nurse,

"Pardon me, but I think someone sent me to the wrong room. That person in there isn't my mother. It's an Asian lady." Alarmed by what she'd seen, she asked, "Could you please direct me to Carroll deCarle's room?"

"That is Carroll deCarle's room," the nurse said.

"No, I can assure you that is *not* my mother in there. Now, please get me to the correct room."

Art noticed the conversation taking place and rushed over saying, "Oh, no. The nurse didn't warn her."

"Courtney?" he said.

"Daddy, thank God. That woman in that room is not Mom. Now where is she?" she asked as she began to cry as if the fabric of her existence had been ripped to shreds.

Art took her in his arms and led her back into the same room explaining as he went, why it didn't look like Mom.

"She's on large amounts of medicine to flush all the poisons from her body and it has drastically increased her size."

"Increased her size is an understatement! My God, She looks like the Michelin Tire Man on steroids. Her eyes are just slits. I thought she was an Asian lady. Why are her arms and legs sticking out to the side? God, she looks so awful."

"That's the fluids being pushed into her body and the poisons beings pushed out. Like a blow up doll with its arms and legs sticking straight out," he said smiling.

"If Mom knew what she looked like she would have heart failure." After realizing what she'd just said, she put her hand over her mouth and cringed. "Sorry mom. *Heart failure* was a bad choice of words." She said, as she moved across the room on unsteady legs, leaned down, and kissed her mother's forehead whispering, "I love you, Mummy. I'm here with Alex and Cam. Barb and Pete picked us up at the airport and they took the boys down to get something to eat." Gently she took her mother's hand as tears slid down her cheeks.

Art slipped out of the room allowing Courtney some private time with her Mom.

"Now you listen to me. The boys and I intend to stay here until you get better. We're not going anywhere. Mac and Jen, Pete and Barb and Daddy have been at the hospital since this morning and none of us are leaving you. So just concentrate on getting better and stop scaring the hell out of everyone. Okay? I'll let you rest now and we'll check back in a little while. I love you. Everyone loves you, you know?"

Courtney bent down and kissed her mother's head before leaving the room. As she got to the doorway, she stopped, turned, and said, "I love you Mummy." She began to whimper softly as she left the room.

Art took her back to the waiting area and everyone talked and cried and told funny stories about growing up with Mom.

They all laughed about her looking like the Michelin Tire Man.

Mac said, "The way her arms and legs are sticking out, they could attach ropes to them and launch her as a new entry in the Macy's Thanksgiving Day Parade."

Everyone broke out laughing and couldn't stop. It was a release of stress, fear, sadness, and all the elements of the day.

`Laughter is indeed the best medicine. And for everyone in that little room, it's exactly what they needed at that very moment, to see things in a different light. A happier and more positive light.

CHAPTER 24

After ninety-six hours on the critical list, I finally broke the cycle to the collective sighs of my family and friends.

They were finally going to move the Michelin Tire Man out of CCU and onto a surgical floor where I could be monitored around the clock. Apparently, I still looked like I would fly away at any moment, but things were improving. Any progress I was making was, indeed, an improvement.

They had me lying on a special bed that continually moved my body for me, keeping up the circulation. It was like magic fingers massaging my entire body all at once. I had a trach tube down my throat and was unable to speak. It would be quite awhile before I was ready to return to the land of the living. Not that I was even aware of my surroundings or where I was. I was heavily sedated for the pain. Even in my brief periods of lucidity, I was not quite sure what was going on. The mere fact that I could see and hear my family and friends was enough. I seemed to drift in and out of consciousness like a shooting star – spectacular, but short-lived.

I had to keep reminding myself that at least I was alive. Or at least I thought I was and that's all that should matter. I would get through this mess. I had already breached an impenetrable fortress called *death*, but emerged on the other side, turning my world around to face a promise to survive no matter what and to discover the world was still waiting for me.

What an incredible revelation! The curtain to my new life was lifting and here I lay center stage . . . tubes, wires, machines, IV's, and all while I smiled inwardly at the strange ostensible purpose of this journey. I managed to discover a viable escape route while battling some strange and silent war. I had looked death squarely in the eye and defied it. I realized that I hadn't done it alone. No, I had a lot of help in that department. Many prayers from family, friends, and people I would probably never have the opportunity to thank. God in all His wisdom, once again, afforded me another chance to live. Will I ever understand all of this? Probably not. But at least I know whom to thank.

As if on cue, a shadow seemed to dissolve out of the wall. Amid the stillness appeared a tall, handsome, white-haired man, Irish smile and all. The true essence of heroism stood before me, the man who saved my life, my friend, my doctor, Dr. Quinn.

Had he arrived in my room that horrible morning at his usual time, I would not have been around to force a smile from my very tired and weakened body. His face was appropriately, the very first face I remembered seeing.

He seemed to notice my struggling to smile and deftly took my hand to reassure me I was still here on earth.

"Welcome back, pretty lady. You are a sight for a lot of sore eyes, I must say. You sure gave us all a hell of a scare," he said with a solemn voice. There was always a quiet dignity about the way he spoke. An ambassadorial-like quality to his stature.

"Your family has been here every day and night since you went back to surgery. I'm going to send them in. I don't want them to wear you out. But they need to see you and you need to see them. Okay? You have the tube in your throat and will for some time. That's why you can't talk. Don't forget it, just know it's there. You're not completely out of the woods yet. But you're peeking your head around the trees and that is a *very* good sign.

"Try and get some rest. I'll be by later." He patted my arm and left to send Art in.

On quiet feet, Art entered my room. With a silence like that which lingers in a church after the service is long over, he appeared by my side. Smiling down at me, this man who'd become the sun about which my whole world revolved, took my hand in his and with glistening eyes said, "Welcome back, Honey. Welcome back."

His smile was as serene as a moon after a rain. A smile and a kiss that reassured me that I was no longer trapped in the branches of evil. Like distant lightning, I experienced a moment of sharp pain, and then it vanished without a trace. As if a summer's rain had momentarily washed away all fear and pain. That smile was like a tonic, restoring my senses. Just hearing his voice was sweet music to my ears. Like a beautiful endless song.

Courtney, Mac, and Jennifer joined Art at my bedside. The smiles on their faces did little to mask the concerns in their eyes. They'd been put through hell this past week forcing them to the narrow ledge of extremes, while their worst fears tightened like a tourniquet on their minds and around their hearts. Here they all stood surrounding my bed like the sea surrounds the shore.

Art said, for everyone's benefit as well as mine, "I think you need to get some rest. We must have worn you out, honey, you look a little tired. We'll be back later." He kissed the top of my head and whispered, "I love you."

In response, I shook my head. Although he detected a slight smile, it failed to transmit it to my eyes where old ghosts lingered.

Everyone kissed me before they left. I soon realized that Art was right. I was tired, but not knowing how tired until everyone was gone and the room grew quiet once again.

My nurse soon arrived with my meds; to change the IV's, hanging one more bag of blood, taking my vitals, and increasing my pain meds. As the pain meds took effect, I slowly slipped into a feeling of euphoria, satisfaction and peace. I relinquished myself to a much needed sleep waiting for my family to arrive once again later that day.

The afternoon arrived and with it brought my family all standing like sentries beside my bed. Having them at my side was my happy pill.

At that point I didn't exactly know what had happened to me, what day it was, or how long I had been here. As I looked at my family's faces, I thought, *what's wrong. Everyone looks like they're mourning the loss of a loved one. Tear streaked faces and smiles that certainly weren't natural. They could smile all they wanted, but their eyes told me a different story. It was like looking into their eyes, but they weren't there. I know they're alive because I felt their lips brush across my forehead as they gently kissed me. I felt them touch my hand, my arm and I felt Courtney brush a strand of run-away hair from my forehead. So they must be alive, right? But what about me? Am I really sure I'm alive, or are they saying their last goodbyes?*

Suddenly fear gripped my heart with a hand of ice striking me paralytic. This feeling of doom floated closer and closer to the surface of my mind. No matter what I did, I could not excise the fear.

I was unable to speak and scarcely able to move because of the pain in my belly and the soft wrist restraints, which I discovered much later were put into place for my own safety. I kept trying to remove my breathing tube and the IV's. I couldn't remember any of this. All I knew was that I was in a blind, whirling panic only able to moan and think. *Would I ever awaken again, to cry or laugh again, to ever know joy or love again? Would Art and I have another chance to grow old together while enjoying watching our children and grandchildren move on with their lives? Why did this have to happen to me? To sleep the sleep that outlasts love. There was that damn "why" again.*

I'm not ready to go. Not yet. I can't. I cried silently as I struggled and moaned.

Why had death shown itself too often in my life? I'm still here and I refuse to go anywhere. God must have something else in mind for me, besides dying.

My family became greatly alarmed with the way I was beginning to act. Art and Mac left in search of a nurse while Courtney and Jen frantically pressed my call button. Alarms were urgently sounding both their cries for help as well as mine.

I lay wild-eyed and in utter helpless horror. The room became alive with voices. Many voices all talking at once.

"What happened?" a nurse cried out to my family.

"We have no idea," Art said, through his mounting fear. "We were all around her bed smiling and talking softly to her and all of a sudden she became agitated. That's all I can tell you."

"I would like everyone to please leave the room so we can do our jobs," one of the nurses said. "We'll let you know when we're through trying to figure this out. Alright?"

"Sure." Art said as he ushered everyone from the room.

Still desperately struggling with fear, I beckoned the nurses for help with my eyes. Eyes as wide as saucers and clouded with tears and desperation.

After giving me a shot to calm me, I slowly began the euphoric journey toward sleep. Praying it wasn't my forever sleep. It couldn't be, could it?"

And then I was gone.

"We think Carroll was frustrated with her breathing tube which caused her inability to speak; plus, the wrist restraints we had to place on her arms," the nurse informed my family upon leaving my room. "All of that probably culminated in her odd behavior. But I'd like her to sleep for now. We've sedated her and she really needs her rest. She shouldn't have any more visitors until this evening. I hope you understand? It's what's best for Carroll; and, I know you want the best for her." The nurse smiled. She looked tired too.

Art arrived later in the day. "Hi, honey. I'm sorry about what happened this afternoon. I've asked the kids to stay home tonight and allow me to visit with you alone. They'll visit tomorrow when you'll probably be up to some company. Today was a little tough for everyone. I hope you're doing better now?" he asked, holding my hand.

I smiled and shook my head, yes. Just having him near was all I wanted or needed. He talked and told me what Alex and little Cam were doing to keep everyone entertained. Those two were precious to me. I loved hearing about them.

Courtney arrived just before Art left to go home. "Hi Mum. I'm going to spend another night in here with you and Daddy can go home and get some sleep. Mac and Jen are taking care of the boys and they're having a great time with their aunt and uncle. I'm so glad they're able to help with the boys, it gives me some alone time to shower, eat, and get a few hours of uninterrupted sleep. I just want you to know that I will not allow anything to happen to you in this damn hospital. Not on my watch. I'm spending every night here so you'll have someone all night long. This way you can sleep peacefully and rest assured that I'm here and I'm not going anywhere."

"Now she knows why we call her the Admiral. Nothing gets by that kid." Art said laughing.

"Thanks." Courtney glanced sideways at her daddy. "I think."

"Don't mention it Honey." Art laughed and gave her a hug.

"Get some rest, Babe." He kissed me goodnight and said I love you.

Before he left the room, he turned back around and smiled at Courtney.

"Did you forget something, Daddy?" Courtney asked, quizzically.

His look was tender, and his eyes filled with regret that she had to see her mother like this. Art walked back toward Courtney, held her and kissed her forehead.

"Is everything okay, Dad?"

"It is now, Honey. It is, now." Still holding her, he said, "Thanks for coming and taking charge. We couldn't have done this without you. I know you've been a great strength for your mother."

"I love you, Daddy."

"Me too, kiddo. Call if you need anything. Now I'm off to a nice shower and a nice soft bed. I'll see you in the morning."

Between Mac, Jen, Barb and Pete, my grandchildren were well-fed, well-loved and well-looked after. Keeping little minds happy, busy, and free of worry was a fulltime operation.

And everyone had it under control.

CHAPTER 25

The days wore on and I was finally moved to my private room. I slowly began to climb that long and very uncertain incline of my life. I had been given an enormous chance to overcome any and all obstacles. As they say, "chance favors the prepared mind."

I had lain supine in my bed, able to do nothing but think for most of each day. I had ample time to prepare my mind, my heart, and my soul for a very long road ahead. I had plenty of time and many one-way conversations with family, friends, doctors, nurses, and therapists. Oftentimes, more than I wanted, but certainly not more than I needed.

As long as my breathing tube was still down my throat, I had nothing to say and everything to hear whether I wanted to or not. Talk about frustration!

One morning my girlfriend, Barb, was visiting. She was seeing to it that I was comfortable as she used a cold cloth on my face and neck. I was trying to get her attention to ask her something, but couldn't because of the tube in my throat.

My newest method of getting attention to those in my room was to tap my fingernails on the rails of my bed. Archaic, but effective, providing the people weren't chattering too loudly.

"What's wrong, Carroll?" Barb asked, ringing out the cloth with fresh water before wiping my hands.

Tap . . . tap . . . tap . . . was all I could muster while trying to convey to her that I needed my pad and pencil.

"Oh! You want your paper and pencil," Barb exclaimed. She got them for me, placed them into my hands, and I began my hen-scratching.

She looked at it with curious eyes, saying, 'You want crackers? You can't eat anything, yet."

Frantically shaking my head *no,* tapping on the pad this time and pointing outside my room in the hall, I tried moaning.

"What is it? I don't understand." Barb said, looking out the door.

Tap, tap, again I went. But she didn't get it.

"Okay, write it again."

After about a dozen times or so, I finally gave up in exasperation.

"I'm sorry, Carroll. I can't read, it. Maybe Art or Mac will when they get here.

Barb sat and chatted with me telling the escapades of Alex and Cam and how everyone was keeping them busy.

Later that afternoon, while Barb was at lunch, Mac arrived.

"Hi, Mum. How are you feeling today? You look much better." He said as be bent and kissed my forehead.

Tap . . . tap . . . tap . . . *Maybe Mac will be able to read my handwriting. He's left-handed and tends to scratch like this. Oh, I hope so.*

"Do you need something?" he asked, before noticing my pencil and pad.

I tapped the pencil on the pad for him to read as I waved my other arm in the air.

"Why are you writing your own name?" He asked perplexed. "I know your name is Carroll. Where's Barb? She'll probably know what you're trying to tell me."

I pretended to be shoveling food into my mouth in an attempt to tell him Barb was at lunch; and also, in a last ditch effort to have him re-read my writing.

"What? She's gone to lunch. You want something to eat? Mum, what in hell are you trying to tell me? Oh, God, where's Barb? She's the only one who can figure this out. Shit!" I heard him say as he turned away from me raking his hands through a head of hair that was growing thinner by the day. I wasn't the only one who was becoming frustrated.

Just in the nick of time, Barb came back into the room carrying a tall paper cup with a lid and straw.

"Hi, Mac. Your mother looks better today, doesn't she?" she said, giving him a hug and a kiss.

"Yeah, she does. But she's been tapping again on her rail and her notepad. I have no idea what she wrote. I think she's trying to write her name. You look at it."

Barb took a look and said, "It could be her name. I told her it looked like she wrote crackers and said she couldn't eat, yet."

"What's going on with her? She's been tapping those damn nails since I got here. Maybe we should call the nurse. What do you think?" Mac asked.

"I guess it wouldn't hurt any." Barb said, and left in search of a nurse to solve the mystery of the *word*.

While Barb was gone, Art arrived and Mac filled him in on the tapping and the mysterious word.

"Hey, there, Missy, I understand you are giving Mac and Barb fits. No one seems to be able to figure out your hen-scratchings," Art said, bending to kiss me.

Thank God Art's here. Maybe he'll understand what I've been trying to ask everyone.

"Let me see your paper," he said, taking the pad from my lap. "Hmm, I can see their dilemma. It's either Carroll, crackers, checkers, or maybe . . . carrots." Art turned the pad in every direction in an attempt to diagnose the malady.

Tap, tap, tap, I started with my fingernails on the bedrail, again.

"Okay," Art said. "Enough with the tapping. I'm doing the best I can, here."

"See what I mean, Dad. That damn tapping is driving everyone nuts. What in hell is she trying to say? I think her meds have sent her to another planet." Mac said, half serious, half not.

I grabbed Art's shirt and tugged. He looked down at me and I pointed at the pad and motioned for him to read it again and read it aloud.

Finally, after figuring out what I was trying to tell him, Barb and my nurse arrived. Now it was a group effort.

You guys would seriously suck at charades, I thought, shaking my head, exhausted.

"Why don't we each say aloud what we think it is and see how she reacts," Art said.

Everyone took their turn, including the nurse. I kept shaking my head *no*. Suddenly, Barb said "carrots?" I nearly flipped out of bed as I shook my head *yes*.

They all looked mystified at one another.

"Carrots? Why do you want carrots? Remember I told you, you can't eat because of your breathing tube?" Barb said, sensing all my frustration while taking my hand.

After what seemed forever, and probably was, Barb finally looked toward what I was pointing at from the other side of my bed and began laughing.

"What?" Mac asked.

"Come stand over here and look at the ceiling above the nurses' station toward the right side of Carroll's doorway." Barb said, moving away from the other side of my bed making room for Art and Mac.

"Carrots! I'll be damned." Mac said, as he and art started to laugh.

I quickly wrote on my pad the word *why*.

Barb laughed and told me why. "It's just a weird shadow above the nurses' station, that's all. No carrots. But, you sure had us all wondering there for a while. Leave it to you to see carrots." Barb bent down and kissed my forehead. I smiled, grateful that I wasn't hallucinating seeing what I thought to be a bunch of carrots hanging outside my door like some unwanted voodoo doll anticipating what spell to cast.

Yes, my days of frustration were many. But, being able to laugh at myself made everything seem just a tiny bit better.

I was happy to have had my pad and pencil. However, there were times I really wished I could have pitched it out the window. I was encouraged to write down my request or thoughts. But most of the time I didn't have the strength to write. A battle of wills was taking place internally and I wasn't winning. I seemed to be fighting a dense tangle of both logical and illogical thoughts. Imperatives disguised as choices. Who did they think they were kidding? Choices? What choices?

Fear engulfed me with great depression. I felt small, lost, and very lonely. More afraid of what they weren't telling me than what they were. And why not? I had every right to be depressed. I had died and was brought back. My heart had stopped and the paddles had to be used to get it beating again. My lungs had collapsed, my kidney's failed. All my organs ceased to function. I battled sepsis as it ravaged my body for nearly twelve hours before anyone paid any attention to me. I was on life support for ninety-six hours. I went through the agonizing pain of having needles inserted into my lungs to remove the fluid that was making it extremely more difficult for me to breathe. I can't tell you how many times that had to be done. It was most excruciating. Oh, you bet I was depressed, angry, and filled with rage.

And I had *way* too many unanswered questions.

CHAPTER 26

It was somewhere around the week of March 18, and my breathing tube had been removed earlier that morning, much to my relief. I had questions that needed answering. Loads of questions which I fully intended to bombard Art with when he arrived. Just how I was going to do that was a horse of a different color. I was having a horrible time just trying to talk. Talking would be a big stretch because the tube had been in for so long and as I would soon discover, when they were rushing me back to surgery they shoved the tube hard enough to separate my vocal chords. I was reassured, however, that I would in time, regain my voice. How could I really begin to believe what these people were telling me? They nearly killed me, these so-called professionals.

Around one P.M., Art popped into my room, took one look at me and his smile froze on his face.

"Oh, oh," he asked. "What's wrong?"

I began moaning and frantically pointing to my pad and pencil, until he eventually realized what I was trying to say. I began scribbling and motioning for him to look at what I'd written. Well, maybe "written" was a bit of a stretch; chicken scratching would be more like it.

I had written, "You tell me?" I tried mumbling something inaudible as I shoved the pad into his hand. My voice was so gravelly that it actually sounded like rocks in a can and not to be understood by anyone but me. I could feel my cheeks becoming warmer by the second.

Art didn't so much as flicker an eyelash to reveal what was hidden behind his eyes. Recovering quickly, he raised his eyebrows, cocked his head, and issued a gentle smile.

I began to gurgle again, waving my hands for him to give me my pad back. I had something else to say, and by George, I intended to say it. Or in my case, scribble it.

"Why is everyone tiptoeing around what's really wrong with me. Tell me, damn it. It's my life and I have a right to know?" I thrust the pad back at him.

While Art struggled to read my hieroglyphics, I watched him intently, looking for any signs of reluctance to answer the question he was reading . . . Or at least attempting to read.

"You're right. It is your life and you do have a right to know. But are you really strong enough to accept it? I don't know. You tell me?" he said, handing back my notepad. He pulled up a chair and sat down. He was forcing me to answer his question.

I could feel the color draining from my face, leaving me a waxen color. I began to tremble. I grabbed my pad and began scribbling. "Oh God, there is something wrong with me."

The tone of Art's voice, more than his words, had really shaken me. His undertone of meaning was unmistakable. An icy silence descended on my room.

I took my pad and began writing. Tears welled up and fell upon the paper. I wept with desolation and sorrow. In a voice inaudibly hoarse and strained with pain, I cried out, "Why?"

Unable to speak any further, I scribbled, "Why is God testing me again? Why?" Strangled sounds of fear and pain struggled to spill from my lips as I released the pad and pencil allowing them to slip silently through the rails of my bed to the floor below.

Art bent down and retrieved them, read what I'd written, and placed them on my bedside table. He leaned over the bed in an attempt to hold me, careful to not disturb my incision or the IV's. In a whisper of a voice he said, "I truly wish I could answer that question. But, honey, I can't; only God can. Maybe one day He'll answer all your *Whys*."

There was a quiet dignity about the way he spoke. A gentleness of words and a sense of reluctance in his voice already tense with emotion. No, there was no triumph in his words.

With a small catch of breath and a voice thin with scarcely a thread of sound, I managed to whisper, "I love you."

With soft but forceful hands, Art gently cupped my face and smiled. "I do love you, too, you know. This isn't the first battlefield we've slogged through. But, just like the others, we'll get through it carrying our flag of victory. I promise you. Now, let me see a smile on that pretty face." He bent down and kissed my lips as tears fell from his eyes.

I tried not to look at him, but my eyes refused to obey. I found myself staring at him with flowing, humble eyes. Total humility etched on my face.

"Promise . . ." My throat would no longer allow my words to emerge. I had him get my pad and pencil and I scratched out what I could not say aloud. "Promise you'll explain everything to me? I can't remember and I'm confused." Fearful thoughts had suddenly been fleshed out with written words.

Before Art could read and answer my questions, after I had timidly broached the subject at hand, I turned slightly away from my poignant appeal. I was experiencing sudden feelings of a mixture of distress, fear, apprehension, trust, and guilt.

Knowing in his heart that complete candor was the only workable course now, Art answered, "I promise. But now I want to see a smile. No more tears. Whatever we have to face, we'll face it together. It's all or nothing. Can you promise that you'll do just that?"

Yes, I nodded, smiling as tears rolled down my cheeks. Eager warmth filled my soul and my heart as it placed a believable smile on my face.

"Good girl. Now, that's the face I've grown to love so much." Art said, already wiping the incidents of today from his mind, mildly content. "I'm going to let you rest, clear your mind and fill it full of happy thoughts. Okay?" He said, kissing my cheek. "Courtney will bring the boys by tomorrow to see you. If you're up to it, that is."

I shook my head *yes* and smiled. Almost on cue and in a flurry, a voice, quickly followed by a nurse, entered the room just in the nick of time. The abrupt silence suddenly reverberating with the decibel sounds of a bubbly, chatty nurse.

Art issued a silent prayer of gratitude for her arrival, said goodbye and he'd see me later, kissed my forehead and departed, leaving me alone with Miss Bubbles and her happy disposition while she delivered my meds through my IV and took my vitals.

As art left the room, he grew somber, quiet, and miserable. Something was gnawing at his insides and for now there wasn't a damn thing he could do about it. He was caught in a spider web of uncertainty threatening to undermine his confidence.

Carroll's implied accusations of not telling her what was wrong were tormenting him and it made him ache inside. Profoundly disturbed by his knowledge of the truth, yet too overwrought to let reason exert a claiming influence on his reasoning, it left him in emotional chaos. Yet, for some unknown reason, he mumbled, "Through all this mess, the goddamn world keeps turning. Go figure!"

When the nurse came out of the room, she suggested Art go home and get some much needed rest. He needed to get away from here for a little while.

"Carroll will be asleep the rest of the day with what I've just given her. She's been through much already today with her breathing tube being removed. Her throat's going to be very sore and raspy for quite a long time, and the more she tries to talk the more damage she's going to do to it. We'd like to keep her as quiet as possible. I have a feeling it's going to be nearly impossible, as she hasn't been able to speak for such a long time. She's got a lot of questions and right now isn't the time for most of them to be answered. Thankfully, she'll be doing a lot of sleeping. But it's for her own good."

Art acquiesced, finding himself longing for the comfort and quiet of his bed. He walked to the bank of elevators, pressed the down button, and stood there alone and thinking. While he waited for the elevator to arrive, he stared out the window and watched as tomorrow's cloud hung heavily over today's sunshine. Shaking his head, he said aloud, "What am I going to do? I'm going to have to tell her everything. How I dread that day. Who in their right mind would have envisioned beginning 2002 on such a shitty note? She wasn't feeling very bad until March.

Will this girl *ever* catch a break?"

Just then the elevator arrived, the doors opened, and Art stepped in with a fiercely heavy heart.

Chapter 27

Now, finally, in my own private room on a floor with all the other patients, I somehow began to feel a tiny bit whole again.

Courtney arrived the next afternoon, just as Art had promised, with two little boys. Alexander, age ten and Cameron age three. Tiny little faces with great big smiles peeked at me through the railing on my bed. This was a moment which transcended all time. A precious moment which seemed transformed to jewels sparkling with the inner-light and innocence of a small child. They were like two little bright birds as they said, "Hi, Nana."

Courtney explained why I couldn't answer them. But I managed a tiny smile and a lift of a finger as an acknowledgement. I could feel my sails swelling full. My room was alive with soft busy feet and tiny running voices. My tear streaked cheeks glistened with joy.

"Why is Nana crying, Mummy?" asked a very perplexed Alex.

"Those are happy tears, Honey. She's so happy to see you and Cammy," Courtney explained.

"We're happy to see her too, aren't we, Cam?"

Cam shook his little head *yes* and with a quiet voice whispered. "Don't cry, Nana."

I forced a smile as Courtney said, "I think Nana should rest awhile now. She looks tired.

We'll see her later. Okay?"

"Okay. Bye, Nana!" they both yelled at the same time and off they went.

"I'll see you later, Mom. Barb is taking care of the boys right now. I'll be back. Love you," she said, as she bent down and kissed my forehead.

I was so happy to see those little faces, hear their voices chattering like magpies. It gave my heart a great sense of joy. I was a lucky lady to have such wonderful family and friends.

I was learning how to slowly walk from my bed to a chair with the aid of two nurses. And when I say slow, I mean really, really slow. Like a snail standing still kinda slow.

I realized my road back sure seemed like it would be a long one. I not only lacked strength, but I lacked coordination. I couldn't get my brain to tell my legs to get moving; and moving in the right direction at the right time. My left leg always seemed to stop while the right one kept going. That made for some very interesting situations.

Something was very odd about this whole therapy thing. Plus, I couldn't seem to remember anything. I was growing more and more frustrated each day. Each time I went to physical therapy, which was twice a day in the beginning, I would return feeling as if I'd accomplished nothing, except more frustration. Sure I was alive, but at what cost.

I couldn't think. I wrote like a child in pre-school. I couldn't remember things as simple as my friends and family's names, or the day of the week. I didn't know who was President. Not that it was that important, because I was sure he wasn't coming for a visit. Heck, I didn't even know what year it was. I couldn't count to ten; and, you could forget counting backward from ten. My hands wouldn't stop shaking. I couldn't seem to control them. I could barely speak. I couldn't walk without falling. I had clots in both lungs which had to be aspirated multiple times. A very painful procedure. I had to endure a speech therapist, a memory therapist, and a physical therapist. I was peeing in one bag attached to a catheter, and pooping in another bag, my ostomy pouch, attached permanently to my tummy, which had to be taken care of by my nurses. I was unable to control the coordination of my hands to do it alone.

I had endured sepsis, two major surgeries in two days, opening my abdomen from above my waist to my groin, twice, leaving me on the critical list for ninety six hours; expected to die.

I had to see kidney specialists, heart specialists, gastroenterologists, laryngologists, lung specialists, ostomy nurses, neurologists, psychologists, and infectious disease specialists. And so many doctors coming and going at all times of the day and night for whatever reason, I really can't say. Quite frankly, I was exhausted, and I'd barely left my bed.

To top it off, if all of that wasn't enough, I had learned I'd had a stroke. Hearing that was nearly the straw that broke the camel's back.

But before I was able to come to grips with the whole stroke thing, my short-term memory loss kicked in and I'd forgotten it as quickly as I'd heard it. That was my only saving grace, I do believe. My short-term memory loss always seemed to kick in at just the right time.

Through it all, I refused to give up. I knew somehow, some way, in time I would be that old Carroll again. I did it before in 1971, and I could do it again in 2002. This time I would have to work a whole lot harder, for a lot of different reasons. But I could do it. No matter how long it took.

On Easter Sunday, March 31, our son and daughter-in-law gave me some really good news. Jen was pregnant with their first child. I was thrilled. I was going to be a grandmother for the third time. Now all I had to do was get better and get out of the hospital. I wanted to be able to hold that tiny life in my arms. I would have about seven months to get into shape. I could do that! I *had* to do that.

Now, if I could just remember why in hell I was working so hard, that would be great. I seemed to be operating on only half a brain cell these days. But I'd press on. I had lots of people who cared. Thank goodness.

Chapter 28

I was released from the hospital on April 4, 2002. I was finally going home. I was apprehensive and fearful that I might not be able to do all the things I was told I'd have to do. I had been safe in my little capsule for so long with everyone doing everything for me on a daily basis. I was nearly paralyzed with fear when I thought about returning home.

A home health nurse would visit me daily for the first few weeks, then once a week until she felt I was doing well enough on my own, with Art's help, of course. I would visit a speech therapist on a daily basis, which helped with my speaking, my memory, cognition, and small motor skills. What small motor skills? Hah! They were non-existent.

I couldn't do a simple child's puzzle; you know the wooden kinds that have little knobs on the pieces enabling a toddler to hold and place the puzzle piece into its proper spot. I would try and try, but I couldn't get my brain to tell my fingers what they had to do and I couldn't get my hands to stop shaking spasmodically. I simply could not pick up those puzzle pieces.

Tears formed a river down my face and neck. My therapist allowed me to cry, held me until the sobbing stopped, and then she said in a gentle voice, "Shall we continue. Let's try one more time. You're doing fine. It'll all come back; we just have to give it time. We can't be impatient. It's not good for you."

"Why do you keep saying *we*? You're not the one who's unable to do anything. *I'm* the one and I'll never get it!" I cried with frustration.

"You're right. Now, let's try again, okay?" she asked quietly.

I wiped my tears, blew my nose, and began again.

All the specialists I had to see while I was in the hospital, I had to continue seeing after I was home and convalescing. I visited the Cumadin Clinic at the hospital, three days a week. I saw my neurologist once a week, the psychologist once a week, as well as the lung specialist, heart specialist, kidney specialist, gastroenterologist, laryngologist, and the infectious disease specialists, all were seen on a weekly basis.

I had my surgical follow-up, and of course, my appointments with my favorite gastroenterologist, Dr. Quinn. My hero. Dr. Quinn was the only doctor I really *didn't* mind seeing.

What a bummer my life was. Art had to get in the shower with me and wash my body and my hair, get me dried off, dressed, take me to my appointments, and fix our meals. That poor soul didn't have a minute's peace. He even had to help me with my ostomy chores.

For just a moment, try and imagine yourself, all of a sudden, not able to tie your shoes, brush your own hair, brush your teeth, button your blouse, zip a zipper, put on makeup, use your silverware, drink from a cup or glass, and so many, many more things we take for granted.

Art would take me, in my wheelchair, outside for some fresh air. I even had to use a wheelchair in my home.

I felt like such a burden to my family and friends. Everyone pitched in and drove me to my various appointments and dropped off meals so Art didn't have to do all the cooking.

Months later, I graduated from a wheelchair to a walker. That was a lot less troublesome. But more physically and mentally challenging for me and a nightmare for Art. He had to continually watch that I wouldn't fall or trip over something including the dogs who wanted to walk along beside or in front of me.

One day while at speech therapy, my therapist informed me that I would have to get used to not being able to read like I used to. I was unable to remember even one word. We had been at this for over six weeks and still I wasn't making any positive progress in the reading arena.

Hearing that was the absolute worst. It was like pounding the final nail in my coffin. My death knell. I had been a voracious reader all my life; now, the best I could manage was to read only one word, and as quickly as I read it, it vanished.

But I persisted on my own. I had to. Reading was the one challenge I had to accomplish.

One afternoon, I picked up a novel, forced myself to read one word, attempting to remember it, refusing to give up until I did. My next step was reading two words, remembering them, and continuing, adding a word at a time, until one day I could actually read an entire sentence. I had finally succeeded. I actually remembered it. *I really remembered it!*

Wow! What a Red Letter Day that was, in more ways than one. If I could read one line, then maybe I could read two and so on.

This little exercise I did faithfully seven days a week for hour upon hour daily, until I was able to read and remember an entire page. It was a long tedious process. In fact, it took me over a year to achieve that goal. But achieve it, I most certainly did. *I had just read and remembered an entire novel.* A Herculean task . . . and I'd finally mastered it.

In the process, I learned something rather important. Something I hadn't known was even possible. I was retraining my brain to do things it had refused to do.

I learned to walk without a walker using only a cane. It took a little over a year, but was quite an accomplishment.

However, I was still at the mercy of family and friends to drive me everywhere. I was unable to drive myself for nearly three years. And for all of you out on those roads during that time, my not being able to drive was a *really, really* good thing. Trust me.

My voice still sounded like a can of rocks. It wasn't until many months later that I learned the reason why it was gravelly. When I was being rushed back to the operating room for emergency surgery that awful day, the breathing tube they used to keep me alive had been forcefully jammed into my throat separating my vocal chords. When I was finally able to talk, I sounded like a frog with a severe case of laryngitis.

To this day, I still have a gravelly voice and I'm extremely prone to coughing spells, which at times are so bad that I can't get my breath and I actually throw up. It's one of those so-called, *injuries of battle*, I guess.

For me, just one of many.

CHAPTER 29

The strangest things happened while I was learning how to live my life over again. I always say that out of something bad, something good emerges. Little did I know that it would take shape in the way of learning how to draw and learning how to write?

I'd never been any good at drawing. I could barely draw a straight line. So why I actually thought I might like to attempt that now when I could scarcely hold any implement in my hand was beyond me.

One day I asked my friend Lisa, who happens to be a very good artist, "How does someone learn to draw who's never drawn anything before?"

Her answer was simple. "Pick up a piece of paper, a pencil and see what you can do."

I fiddled around a couple of weeks attempting to draw a picture of an old barn. One day I called her, she ran over, took one look at it, and said, "Wow! That's pretty good."

The next thing I knew she presented me with an artist's drawing pad and a large assortment of artist's pencils. I was really excited now. I worked and worked at drawing everything from animals to people to buildings to harbor scenes. Plus, I kept improving on the drawing of my old barn.

Each day I would call her. And each day Lisa would run over, give me ideas and praise for what I was doing. And my wheel kept spinning.

I found a snapshot of my baby grandson, Trey, and used it as a model for a pencil sketch. When I finished I called Lisa and she and her husband arrived, took one look, and couldn't believe their eyes. I had actually drawn a life-like picture of Trey.

They weren't the only ones who were astounded. I was so busy drawing that I hadn't taken the time to actually sit back and examine at my work. It really was pretty good. I was so proud I could have burst, especially when Lisa told me how good it was. I couldn't believe my ears.

Not one to rest on her laurels, I pressed on. I found a snapshot of Art on the wing of his Navy plane wearing his flight suit and holding his flight helmet. I spent nearly six weeks trying to capture that moment on paper. I succeeded.

I was absolutely amazed at my ability to draw the darn thing, even with all the apparatus in the planes' cockpit and on Art's flight suit, including his flight helmet with its attached oxygen mask, face shield, and a myriad of wires attaching it to the inside of the plane. But I'd done it.

My next attempt was a portrait of Art's father. Gee, I was on a roll and Lisa and Patrick were there every step of the way encouraging me to keep it up. I'd kept my sketches from Art, Mac, and Jennifer. I wanted to surprise them.

When I'd completed the three pictures, Lisa encouraged me to have them framed and presented as gifts. She drove me to the art shop where we left them. We picked them up a week later, brought them home and we wrapped them.

Mac received the one of his grandfather. Jen, the one of Trey. And Art, the one of him on the wing of his plane. It was a very proud moment for me to see the smiles on their faces as they opened their gifts. I was not only having a great time, but I was learning how to make my mind and my hands work again. They were learning new and exciting things.

These hands of mine have learned many things since the debacle in 2002. Not only did they learn how to draw, but they learned how to use a computer. For all of you who know me personally, you know what a challenge that was. First of all, I'd sworn I would never, under any circumstances, go anywhere near a computer. I tried it once in the early 1980's and it was a fiasco.

Art signed me up for lessons in a beginner's class at the local computer store. I will tell you that I did it under protest. Lots of protesting, right up to the day that I left home for my first beginner lesson.

I must admit, I was quite nervous because I had only learned from Art how to turn the thing on. That was it. It would be their job to teach me anything else.

Oh, boy was I in for a rude awakening. I was the only person in the class who was an actual beginner, a *real beginner*. Every time I raised my hand to ask another question, the instructor would say, "Since you seem to have so many questions, I suggest you hold them 'til the end of the class and then I'll answer them."

"Hold them 'til the end? What was she saying? I wouldn't remember what they were by the end of the class."

Finally, I couldn't stand it any longer and my frustration won out. I asked her, "I thought this was supposed to be a beginner's class. The only one in here who's a beginner seems to be me. What's up with that?"

"Well most people have at least some knowledge of what they're doing with their computer before they come here."

"Well, I want you to know that I intend to get my money back. The next time you advertise a class as a *beginner's*, I might suggest that it actually be a beginner's or at least explain in detail what a beginner's class entails."

I got up, took myself and my word perfect manual, promptly marched out of the classroom, jumped into my car, and drove home ready to strangle Art.

When I entered the house, he took one look at me and knew something had happened and it probably wasn't good. "Okay, what's wrong?"

"Everything. That beginner's class you signed me up for was anything but. I was the only one in the room who hadn't a clue as to what was going on. They already knew how to use a computer. I barely remembered how to turn it on. That's it!" I said gritting my teeth. "You know what you can do with your computer, don't you. Forget it. I'll never be embarrassed like that again. You can drag me kicking into the twenty-first century if you like, but I'll never go near a computer again. And you can't make me."

I was furious and really embarrassed. I felt like the world's biggest dummy. If I ever decided to use a computer, which was highly unlikely at this point, I would do it on my own.

Well that day came. I did learn to use a computer. And I learned to use it on my own, with a little help from Art. One day in 2009, I said to Art, "I'm going to write a book. A murder mystery. And guess what I'll need? A computer."

"Really! What makes you think you can write a murder mystery. How many have you written before now?" There was a hint of sarcasm in his voice.

"What's that got to do with anything? I've read thousands over my lifetime. I think that should qualify me to be able to write one. You don't actually have to murder someone to be able to write a good murder mystery. Shoot, it can't be that difficult. Have you read some of the stuff those writers write? Not all that terrific, if I say so myself.

"Also, everyone had to start at the beginning and so am I. I just need a computer to put my novel on. I'm going to write it all by hand first. So I'll need lots of spiral notebooks and pencils and those little flag thingies that you can stick on something of interest."

"What's this book going to be about?" Now he was curious.

"I'm in the process of figuring that out now. But it'll have lots of interesting people, places, and things. Interesting plots of murder and mayhem. Sex! I can do it. I learned to draw. So why not learn to write."

"Shouldn't you consider taking a writing class first? You'll learn a lot of what you'll need to write your book."

"Nope. I don't need a class. I need to get on this thing. It'll be really good therapy for me. I'll have to use my brain. My fingers will be put to the task of writing my words on paper and them typing them onto the computer. Yeah, it'll be really good therapy. So, what do you say? You wanted me to learn to use a computer, so here I am. Asking for your help."

"Okay. I'll order you a computer and I'll help you get you started."

"Terrific!" I said, scrambling to find some note books and pencils.

That's exactly how I began my writing career. Well, perhaps *career* is a tad too pretentious. It took me several years of writing my novel, re-writing it, and using my friend Lisa, to help me through some difficult times. And there were loads of difficult times. Times when I'd thought I'd lost the entire book when I inadvertently hit a wrong key on my new computer and everything disappeared.

Cries of help went out across my phone line and Lisa came padding over at six A.M. one morning to fix my goof-up; pink bathrobe, slippers, and hair going in all different directions. Now, *that's* what I call a friend. Even though she looked like she'd been dragged through a knothole backwards, she still came to the aid of her wounded warrior.

It turned out not to be as bad as I thought. She discovered what I'd done and remedied the situation in just a few clicks of a key. That girl's one smart cookie.

I was now back in the old saddle, on my horse, and ready to ride off into another sunset. As long as Lisa was only a phone call away, I'd be just fine. I'm so fortunate in having an award winning renowned travel writer as a mentor. She's one terrific writer and one terrific friend.

Lisa went above and beyond. She always had time for me no matter how busy she was. I'll forever cherish those middle of the night jaunts she made across the street to help out her helpless friend.

She's been my inspiration in doing things I didn't know I could do. She helped immensely with the writing of my first book. I would read sections to her and she would critique it for me openly and honestly. When it was finally finished, I e-mailed her a copy. I was a little hesitant because Lisa isn't exactly crazy about murder mysteries. That's not the kind of book she would read. So I held my breath and waited.

She became so engrossed in the story; she nearly forgot to feed her dogs. But like any good dog, they kept barking until she got their message. They were hungry and they weren't about to let her forget it. They didn't care whose book she was reading.

Yes, out of something bad, something good always finds a way to break through. And many good things have happened to me. Learning to draw, learning to write, and learning to use a computer. All positive things to help me on my journey.

So it took me a couple of years to learn how to do each. So what? I did it and didn't sweat the small stuff. I pressed on.

No matter how large or how small your step, progress is progress. I learned from my mistakes. And, boy of boy, did I have mistakes! A gazillion mistakes, at least. Would I make more mistakes in the future? Absolutely. Would I learn from them? Absolutely. And my friends, so will you.

Each time I learn a new lesson, I have enhanced my chances of a longer, more fulfilling, and rewarding life.

Could *you* do these things when you were told you couldn't? When your body wouldn't allow you to take another step. Or to think or read one more word. Or to remember things you just heard minutes ago, and have now forgotten. I can't answer that for you. Only you can. But I can tell you this. If you are willing, both mind and body, and your attitude is screwed on straight, you can accomplish almost anything you tackle. I did, and I'm not that special. I just refused to give up or give in. Life is too great to let it pass you by. Enjoy every minute. You don't know when it may be your last.

CHAPTER 30

I owe such a debt of gratitude to those who did everything they could to ensure I got better. My family. My friends. Friends, who really have become my family.

But, there is one friend in particular who spent years of countless hours driving me back and forth to hospitals and doctors appointments lifting the burden off the shoulders of Art and the kids.

My girlfriend, Pattie Meades, gave of herself in a most generous, selfless, and compassionate manner. Never once, did she complain. Nor, would she allow me to. When she noticed I was unable to cut my food one day at lunch, she quietly took over the task as she talked on about her morning at the gym. She'd never call attention to the fact that I couldn't do a simple thing like cut my own food. She also encouraged me to join her gym and to hire a personal trainer who specialized in people with disabilities. I couldn't get out of going, because she was my driver. Pattie made going to the gym fun and in doing so, I grew stronger. I thank her for making me do things I didn't think I was able to do. Pattie and my daughter Courtney are very much alike. Neither one will take *no* for an answer and they are relentless. In my case, that was a really good thing. Pattie truly was a godsend.

At home, Art would take care of those tasks for me. Things I had taken for granted all my life, were now obstacles I had to face everyday. The pressures of what I could no longer do, of what I wanted and needed to do, and the realization that I might *never* be able to do these things again, were slowly infiltrating every fiber of my being.

There were so many days I felt like throwing in the towel, giving up all hope. I was exhausted and didn't think I was accomplishing anything. And I didn't care. I would take one step forward and three steps back. There were days when I would cry and cry and cry, alone, not wanting Art to see or hear me. I questioned why I was killing myself, forcing myself to do things my body had no interest in doing. It was the height of lunacy. Doing the same things over and over and expecting different results. I was angry, despondent, full of shame and racked with guilt. But guilt needed some soil in which to grow. I was not only providing the soil, I was providing its nutrients. I was feeding and overfeeding to the point where it had become nearly impossible to control.

Why? There was that damnable question again. The one I couldn't answer years ago and still couldn't. Or was it simply that I was too fearful of the answer. All I really knew was that there were at least three different heads on my shoulders and each one seemed to be screaming a different answer, offering a different directive. My mind danced frantically searching for the right road, afraid to give up, but afraid to move on. I was stuck in limbo, praying I would make the right decision.

But was there truly a right or wrong decision to be made? How could I possibly know, I'd never traveled this road before. And, I was traveling it blindly without a roadmap. I was lost and had no idea how to find my way back.

My therapists could only do so much to help. In fact, no one could take this journey but me. It was one I must take and take alone. I came to realize that all that help from family and friends was in preparation of this long, lonesome expedition of mine. Its end result would have to come from me and only me. Was I mentally tough enough to battle through all the roadblocks which lay ahead? I would never know until I started. All I kept thinking was *what if it works and you don't try?*

It was at that precise moment that all the positive thinking phrases seemed to flood my mind and all at once. *If you can believe it, you can achieve it. If it is to be, it's up to me.* On and on it went.

It was then that I understood I could no longer allow negative feelings to descend upon and invade my thoughts like some demonic incubus.

No, it was time for this timid David to pick up her slingshot of faith, belief, and trust, and strike down the mighty Goliath who'd towered over her every sense of logic for way too long.

I was suddenly possessed with this dizzy, powerful feeling of victory. Instantly, I knew I would win my battle. I would do whatever it took to succeed. And I *would* succeed.

That same old question popped into my mind. *Why?* All I knew was I didn't care *why*. I just knew I would. No longer would I have those lingering stranded, left-behind feelings. I was moving on and nothing was going to prevent my having a successful culmination to a long, rocky journey. My road would be smooth. Sure, some unexpected potholes and detours would surface along the way. That would be inevitable. But I would do whatever it took to circumnavigate around them.

My joyful heart thundered like a herd of wild mustangs racing across the plains. Heads high, manes feathered in the breeze, their spirits free to run like the wind. Free to simply . . . *be!*

I felt as though some unbearable burden had been lifted from deep inside. From the darkest corners of my life. There would be no more shadows of sadness lurking.

There would always be that question, *Why,* hovering about. But, just because there was a question, didn't always mean there was an answer. Life would be full of questions without answers. But if life always presented us with her answers, we wouldn't continue to ask her questions. There would be no challenges to make us stronger, to exercise our minds. It's often in the asking of a question that we find our answer.

All I knew was that my tomorrows would never be the same again. And I would be eternally grateful to God for once more taking my hand and leading me to the right pasture. The winds of fortune promised to carry me in new and astounding directions, experiencing new and astounding things. Opening doors without needing to know what was on the other side, just knowing and wanting to step through and discover what life had to offer, was enough.

Deciding to spend the rest of my life in the future, instead of the past; but understanding that because of the past, I have a future. The past was lessons learned, lessons pressed between the pages of my life to be looked back upon with deep and meaningful reflection. Like the flower you placed between the pages of a book for all time. Gone, but not forgotten. Preparing to face life with a new fresh sense of direction, while unraveling your destiny, merely realizing that your past needn't be simply a diminishing road, but rather an enormous spring meadow upon which no winter shall ever descend.

We can't buy back our yesterdays. But, we can invest in all our tomorrows, no longer willing to allow life to slip away like sand through our fingers. We can't live our lives like a funnel attempting to channel everything through it. But live life as if borne on a gentle fragrant breeze floating serenely on soft drifting clouds through a free and limitless expanse into vast distances beyond all that separates here from there. The ability to set aside selected parts of our past so they don't get in the way of our future.

I remember those times vividly, like they were an old photo album whose pages became worn and dog-eared over time. For me, getting lost in the past meant surrendering to my future and I refused to raise a white flag. My battle was far from over.

THE PRESENT - 2017

CHAPTER 31

As I told you in the beginning of my book, I would tell you about the day my *Why* was answered. But in order to get you to this point I had to take you back to 1971 and bring you through 2002, and to now 2017.

It was important for you to have participated in my journey, because perhaps you are or know of someone who is suffering from Crohn/ Colitis, IBD, an ileostomy, colostomy or a urostomy.

If so, I hope you are able to now understand how they are indeed suffering and mostly suffering in silence.

I spent so much of my life asking myself, *Why? Why me?* But I had to keep asking God because I knew one day when He was ready for me to know the answer to my *Why*, hopefully, I'd be ready to hear Him, and perhaps even understand why it took so long.

Well it was answered, alright, but, not quite the way I had hoped or would have ever expected. In fact, it caught me completely off guard and threw me into a tailspin. One which I wasn't sure I would ever recover from. Somehow I knew I had no choice but to recover.

In October, 2011, my *Why* was answered in the oddest of ways. It came in the form of my eldest grandson, Alexander deCarle West.

Alex, a junior at the University of Arkansas, Fayetteville, had been complaining off and on of abdominal cramping and nausea for several months now. Somewhere in a dark corner of my mind something kept reminding me to mention Crohn's to our daughter, Courtney. After all, she was more than familiar with the disease. But everyone thought it was probably just the added pressures of the load he was carrying at school; plus, his fraternity was going through Rush Week, and he was going in ten directions at once. Understandable, I guess. I accepted those reasons. Also, the added pressure of his parents divorce the past year certainly didn't help. It was a lot to heap on someone's shoulders, no matter how old they were. Art and I kept our fears right where they were. Here in Sarasota, in a far corner of our minds. For now, at least.

Between Thanksgiving and New Year, 2012, he still wasn't much better and his doctor prescribed various meds but none seemed to be doing the trick. He couldn't eat, suffered from copious bouts of vomiting, diarrhea, and had lost so much weight I almost didn't recognize him.

One December evening, Courtney had to rush Alex to the local hospital because of his pain. He was there overnight, a series of tests were performed and it was determined that he could be suffering from Crohn's disease. The meds they started him on seemed to work only for a short while.

After New Year's, he returned with the rest of the students to the University of Arkansas and his Fraternity House, Sigma Nu, where he'd been living. January, 2012, didn't prove to be much better for Alex. He was still in a lot of pain, vomiting, diarrhea, and he was losing more weight.

Courtney made an appointment with a different gastrointestinal specialist. This time she had found a really good doctor in Fayetteville where Alex attended college. Both Alex and Courtney seemed pleased with their new doctor and his new regimen for Alex. His prognosis seemed a little brighter. We were all delighted.

But, for me, I'd pictured a far different scenario than just being delighted. Having suffered with Crohn's for probably most of my teenage years, but not knowing what it was in those days, the early 1950's. It seemed that each time I had a test in school I would have diarrhea and stomach cramps. I chalked it up to nerves, to an excuse of being a nervous wreck before and during a test. I just didn't test well. A lot of people don't test well. It was as simple as that. What else could it be? So I thought.

It wasn't until after the birth of Courtney in 1966 that I was misdiagnosed with having what the doctors thought was colitis. The rest you already know ... Crohn's disease and an ileostomy.

CHAPTER 32

A lex began feeling nauseous, extremely tired to the point where all he wanted to do was sleep. He couldn't keep any food down and the severity of his pain increased. This continued through all of January, February, and half of March.

Alex and Cameron had planned to spend their spring break here in Sarasota, with Art and me. However, because of Alex's illness, everyone thought it best not to attempt the trip.

Alex returned to Fayetteville after his spring break, on Sunday, March 25. At four A.M., our time, March 26, Courtney called and said Alex had been hospitalized in excruciating pain. He was driven to the hospital by his fraternity brothers and she was on her way to be with him.

Art and I grew very uneasy thinking of her driving an hour and a half to the hospital all alone. Knowing Courtney, she was probably crying and speeding. Not a very good combination. But being a mother, I fully understood how she felt. I'm sure it was the longest one and a half hours of her life.

After several tests, and a healthy infusion of morphine in his IV, Alex was at least feeling more comfortable. In fact, I'm quite certain, he was probably feeling *nooo* pain at all.

Courtney arrived safely at the hospital at 4:30 A.M. After being told where her son was, a nurse escorted her to the emergency room. Here they would wait for the test results and to see his doctor when he arrived at the hospital within the hour.

Just as they were waiting for the doctors to assess Alex's progress or lack of, Art and I were doing precisely the same thing, waiting here at home.

After Courtney's phone call at four A.M., there would be no more sleep for two worried grandparents. I was nearly beside myself, sick with worry. I knew exactly what that young man was going through. In fact, I was the only one who could appreciate his pain. His fears. And the many uncertainties running through his head. I had been there, exactly where he was. As frightened as he undoubtedly was, I was doubly frightened.

I kept thinking of all the *what ifs*. And believe me, there were plenty, far too many to wrap my head around. But the biggest *what if* that kept running through my mind, like the continuous loop running at the bottom of your television screen, was *what if he has to have an ileostomy?* That was by far my worst fear. If he had to have that surgery, I was going to be on the next plane out. There would be no stopping me. I had made up my mind.

Courtney kept us informed often. We waited all day. Finally around 2:30 P.M., the phone rang and Art and I both jumped to get to it. "Courtney? What's happening?"

I was having difficulty hearing Courtney because Art was yelling, "Put her on speaker, for God's sake. I need to hear this too."

Not thinking about speaker when I picked up, I quickly hit the button so both of us could hear what Courtney was saying.

"Mom, I'm so scared." We could hear the trembling in her voice and knew she was crying.

"Exactly what did the doctors tell you, Honey?" Art asked, not sure he was ready to hear her answer.

"They're going to have to do emergency surgery in three hours. The latest tests showed what appeared to be bowel loops and two fistulas on his intestine. It was also determined that they would undoubtedly have to remove about six inches of his small intestine. I'm scared to death." Courtney began sobbing uncontrollably.

"I know you are, Honey. But everything will be okay. I promise you. Alex is young and he's strong. Plus, we don't really know yet, what they'll have to do." I tried to put her mind at ease, but knew it would be impossible.

"How can you possibly promise me that everything will be okay? You don't know that." I could not only hear the fear in her voice, but I felt the full force of her fear and anger at me for saying something I had no business saying.

Courtney was right, how could I possibly know he would be alright?

"Honey, you're absolutely right. I had no right promising that. But, with what I've gone through in the past, God has never let me down. And, Courtney, I know He won't let Alex down either. Don't ask me how I know. I just know.

"I also know they probably have a chapel in the hospital, I suggest you visit it and ask God for His help. He never lets us down. This I *can* promise you."

"I'll find it. Mom, what is a fistula. The doctor told me, but my brain didn't seem to be paying attention. I can't remember what he said."

"A fistula is an abnormal channel that may drain outside the body or into the body. Sometimes it will perforate the abdominal cavity, and infections tend to spread quickly. This is probably why they're getting him to surgery so fast. This is a good thing. Speed is his friend right now. Believe me. The surgeon seems to know his business. I'm really glad to hear he's prepping Alex for surgery."

"But, Mom, when you say infections, is that the same as what you went through in 2002?" she asked, as fear crept into her voice filling her with a sense of uneasiness.

"Not necessarily. That's why they're hurrying up. They'll do immediate exploratory surgery in order to locate and drain the abscess as well as wash out the abdominal cavity.

"In Alex's case, they've already alluded to the fact that they'll probably have to remove some of his small intestine. That's nothing more than removing the diseased section and reattaching the two remaining ends, stitch him up, and send him to recovery."

"Are you sure?" she asked, as a terrifying cloud of doubt hovered above.

"As sure as I can be for now, Hon. I'm just sorry I can't be there with you. Daddy and I are only able to provide you with assurances and love over the damn phone. That really bothers us. Are you alone?"

"No. Alex's fraternity brothers have been keeping me company. David will be here shortly with Cameron."

"I'm glad someone is there with you. Is there anything Daddy and I can do for you?" I asked, my heart aching.

"Please call Mac. I need to talk to him." Courtney said through a flood of tears and anguish.

"We'll do it right now, honey." Art said, his voice cracking. "I wish we could be there for you. But, please listen to Mom. No one knows any more about what Alex is going through than your mother. Try and get a little rest. I know I'm probably talking to the wind, but we don't need you to get sick. Get something to eat. You'll need your strength. Okay?"

"Okay, Daddy. Call Mac, now. Please!"

"We will. We love you, Honey. Call when you know something else or just to talk. We'll be here. We're not going anywhere." Art said.

"I love you, baby girl." I said. "Get something to eat. We'll talk later. Bye, bye."

"Bye, you guys. I love you."

"We love you too. Bye, bye." We both said into the phone and then the connection was broken.

What an empty feeling that was. The silence was nearly deafening as neither said anything for what seemed an eternity. Each lost in his own thoughts.

"Why don't you call Mac, now?" Art said, breaking the uncomfortable silence.

"Good idea." I said as I began dialing our son's number. I was able to reach him and he said he'd immediately call his sister.

Now we wait . . .

CHAPTER 33

Courtney let us know that Alex was in holding, waiting for the operating room to be ready. He's had something for his pain and everyone is on pins and needles, waiting. His surgeon told them it would
be about a one and a half hour surgery.

Art and I waited anxiously for the phone to ring with Courtney telling us that they finally took him in. It's now seven P.M., our time. Six,
theirs. The clock ticks so slowly when you are in a hurry. It was like
the slowness of molasses dripping on a cold day.

As if blasted out of our reverie, the phone rang, and we nearly
jumped out of our skin. It was Courtney.

"Quick, put her on speaker!" Art yelled, as I grabbed for the phone.

"He just went into surgery. Oh, Mom, he looked so small. David,
Cam, and I were there when they rolled him out of holding. It's killing
me. I feel like I'm floating on a log, alone, and adrift somewhere far
away." Courtney cried into the phone.

"Okay. Now buck up. There's nothing to worry about. I know
you've been through hell and back so many times with me. But let that
be a platform for you. Alex will be fine. Think about how strong you
were for me when I needed you. You'll be just as strong for Alex. You're
a warrior, Court. There is no one as strong as you. God gave you those
strengths for a reason.

Use them. You have to take care of Alex and Cameron and yourself.
We know you can do it. And we know you *will* do it. You have to do it.
Use your talents and you'll get through this. "Look at what you've had
to plow through this last year. Yours is the strength those boys draw
upon. Don't let them down. You're the best mother there is. They have
no idea how lucky they are to have you. I know firsthand, how special
you are. I've known from the day you helped save my life when you
were only five years old. When I was too sick to take care of myself,

you picked up the reins and took control. You called the neighbors and got help. You tried to console me while your little heart must have been breaking. I know you were frightened beyond belief, but you pressed on like a little soldier. There's no one as strong as you, Courtney. You'll get through this and so will Alex. Trust me. Trust and believe in yourself. Go now and visit the chapel. Take Cameron with you. Daddy and I'll do our part here asking God to be with Alex. But, you guys need to do the same thing out there. Okay?"

"Okay. I'll call you as soon as we hear something from the surgeon. And Mum, I'm spending the night with Alex. I don't want what happened to you to happen to him. Love you guys. Bye now."

"We love you too and we're glad you'll be spending the night with Alex. It'll be comforting for all of us. Call us, love you. Bye, bye."

"Shit!" Art said, as he sat back in his chair.

"I know. I know." I said sinking into my seat. "They're so far away. So far away."

I looked out the window and watched as daylight slowly blended into nightfall. Moving like a slow river flowing into the hollow of a failing day.

Hope. That thing that springs eternal. Life was a crap shoot. With the simple roll of the dice, your life could become a thing of beauty or a great big load of shit. Pardon the pun.

When I was told in December, that my grandson had Crohn's, I was devastated to say the least. And once again, I found myself with a lonely companion . . . guilt! I felt like a sailboat trying to sail on yesterday's wind. Lost.

Even though the cause of Crohn's is still unknown, there appears to be a genetic link, as the disease is more common in those having relatives with Crohn's. Approximately 20% of those diagnosed, have a blood relative with an IBD (irritable bowel disease). If that relative is a sibling, their risk of developing Crohn's is thirty times higher than the general public. Rates are higher in smokers than non-smokers.

Although the cause is still unknown, one of the most popular theories is that in a patient with Crohn's disease, the immune system reacts abnormally, mistaking bacteria, and unknown virus or other substances occurring in the bowel, as being a foreign invader. The immune system's job is to attack and remove these *foreign* objects. This causes an increase in white blood cells in the lining of the intestines which leads to the inflammation associated with Crohn's.

Once the immune system has been *turned on*, the command to switch it off appears to be neglected, causing your body to attack itself.

Scientists have many theories regarding Crohn's as being caused by infection or diet. To date there has been no evidence that either is the cause.

Although once thought to be a factor, research has ruled out stress, tension, and anxiety as causes for an IBD. Stress and anxiety are not the cause of Crohn's, but high levels of either may aggravate the symptoms. To dispel another misnomer, Crohn's Disease is *not* contagious. I just thought I'd set the record straight on that little piece of information.

Chapter 34

I had a lot of time the day of Alex's surgery, to reflect upon his journey from birth to this trying moment in his life of nearly twenty one years old. As I reflected, I could feel and hear my heart begin to break. I didn't believe that you could actually *hear* your heart break, but believe me, you can indeed. It's a terrifying feeling. One I wish never to experience again.

So many memories of Alex came flooding back to me that awful day; being played over and over, as if someone pressed the rewind switch in my brain.

Alex and I have a very special bond. It was formed the day I first laid eyes on that tiny body as he lay in an incubator in Washington Regional Hospital, Fayetteville, Arkansas. It seems so strange to me how he has come full-circle and is yet again lying helplessly in distress in the same hospital in which he was born. Alex was a preemie and had to be in an incubator for three weeks before he could go home.

After he was released from the hospital, he had to be hooked up to a baby apnea monitor. He wore an apparatus around his midsection with electrodes and wires attached to a unit which had to go everywhere he went. It would emit a piercing alarm when his breathing stopped.

We all had many sleepless nights. Every time the alarm went off, people scrambled to his parent's bedroom, where he slept, in case they failed to hear the screeching alarm. Highly unlikely that you would ever miss hearing *that* noise. That thing was so loud I'm sure you could have heard it in another county. He was attached to that alarm for more than six months.

When Alex was strong enough to travel, he and his parents followed Art and I from Fayetteville, Arkansas, to Sarasota. Our home was where they would live while David went through flight school.

It was in those two years, that I formed a strong, unbreakable bond with my tiny grandson. A bond that I'll never have with any other grandchild. And that's because Alex was the only grandchild to ever live in our home.

Please don't get me wrong. I love each of the four equally and yet in very different ways. However, Alex is the one I have a vibrant connection to.

He was a really fortunate baby. He was living in a home with both parents, his grandparents, his great-grandmother, his uncle Mac, and two dogs. Oh boy, did we spoil that little one. Spoiling him in a good way. He had more attention and love than anyone could imagine.

I loved those days with my first grandchild. Those days when nothing mattered but watching him grow on a daily basis before our very eyes. Being a part of his first . . . everything. Yes, they were really special times for everyone. But especially for me. They were like poetic moments once again brought to life by a tiny baby. Those months I'd spent at the Mayo Clinic were like lost chapters of my life which I knew would never be recaptured. Time was an element which could not be hoarded and the pages of my life kept turning. I'd been robbed of so many precious memories of my son, Mac. The day he said his first word, to hear him call my name, *Mama*, to see him crawl and then to watch as he took his first steps on unsure legs. But, God granted me another chance to enjoy all the things I'd missed with Mac. He gave me Alex. It saddens me deeply as I reflect upon those lonely days of not being there for my baby. But God gave me a second chance to relive those lost moments through my grandson's first miracles. I cling to those memories as I would a life preserver in a stormy sea. Very grateful for a second chance to remove all shadows from my heart.

Alex is a young man with a rare gift of compassion, humor, love, understanding, intelligence, selflessness, friendship, and deep, almost mystical patience with me. He is calm, capable, and most of all, considerate. He has profoundly enriched my life.

Alex and I will forever have this unspoken bond between us.

CHAPTER 35

As difficult as it was for me having to wait for news of Alex's surgery, I can only imagine the degree of difficulty my daughter was experiencing. Once again she was forced to deal with horrible situations that no one should be forced to confront and yet try and make rational sense of. Her early childhood memories of her mother being so sick for so long at so many times in her life, first when she was nearly five, again when she was thirty six, and now when she's in her mid forties, are more than anyone should have to endure.

This time her picture had drastically changed. She's now praying for the successful outcome of her first born son's surgery. The terror of these months of watching him go through horrific pain and sickness, and now surgery, have culminated in something dark that seems to be hovering over all of us like the haunted limbs of a long dead tree.

A lifetime of memories boiled down to many long hours of waiting. Long, lonely hours of simply waiting, as our minds disappear down some long endless corridor of the past. Unsure of what the future has in store for Alex, while putting all our faith in the hands of God to guide the surgeon to a skillful and positive outcome seemed to be our only option.

Prayer is a powerful opiate. As long as we believe in God's strength, wisdom and His love, we'll be just fine. Alex will be fine. God will hear our prayers and make Alex whole once more to go on to do great things with his life. I feel this to my very core!

I would gladly change places with my grandson if I could. Of this, I'm very sure. But that was not my choice to make, unfortunately.

Two families, sat hundreds of miles apart, pacing, crying, thinking, and trying to distract their troubled minds to anywhere but where they were. To what they were thinking and feeling, searching for any sign that our world would remain stable as our minds danced to the erratic dictates of fear.

Someone once told me that as a parent you try as hard as you can. You somehow love beyond all reason, no matter the circumstances. You fight with all you have to endure what you must. And you hope beyond all hope, believe beyond all belief. And never once do you think, until the very last moment, that given all your efforts, it still may not be enough.

The doors opened and in walked Alex's surgeon. Dressed in his surgical scrubs, he removed his doo-rag from his head, and as it dangled in his hand, a smile crossed his lips. Everyone in the waiting room jumped to their feet, each filled with mixed emotions. The doctor was smiling, but was that only because he was being kind and really had bad news?

"He's out of surgery and doing well. It only took fifty minutes instead of what we predicted earlier. The hour and a half. He's being moved to recovery and as soon as he's all set up and settled, you can go in to see him."

"Thank you, doctor." Courtney said, as her tear streaked cheeks glistened with joy.

"Yes, thanks doctor." Alex's dad, David, said shaking hands with the doctor.

Cameron, Alex's younger brother, grabbed his mom's hand and said, "He's gonna be okay, mom." His own eyes blurred with tears.

"What did you find?" Courtney asked. "Is it Crohn's?"

"What we found was astonishing. It's called Meckel's diverticulum."

Courtney and her ex-husband, David, looked at each other, frowning, and asked, "What is that?"

"I've never heard of that before." Courtney said, bewildered by what she'd heard.

"Why don't we all sit down and I'll attempt to explain it."

Everyone took a seat and the doctor began his explanation of this strange new thing he'd discovered.

"Meckel's diverticulum is a pouch on the wall of the lower part of the intestine that is present at birth. The diverticulum may contain tissue that is identical to tissue of the stomach or pancreas."

"What causes this?" Courtney asked.

"It's tissue that's left over from structures in the unborn baby's digestive tract that were not fully reabsorbed before birth. Approximately only two percent of the world's population has a Meckel's diverticulum, and only a few people *ever* develop symptoms. Those symptoms quite often occur during the first few years of life, but may not start until adulthood. As in Alex's case."

"Good God," Courtney said.

"Alex presented some of the symptoms in his abdominal pain. Very few surgeons, in their lifetime, ever see this Meckel's. It's truly astounding."

"What's the treatment?" David asked.

"That's already been taken care of. A segment of his small intestine that contained it was removed, and the ends of the intestine were resected. He should make a full recovery. We're not anticipating any complications. But for the rest of his life, he'll probably need B-12 shots. But that's about all."

"What about the Crohn's?" Courtney quickly asked, not hearing the doctor say anything about it.

"I can't answer that just yet. We've sent the Meckel's to pathology and we'll have the results in a few days. So until then, we won't know. But your son's doing fine. That's the main thing right now."

"Thanks, doctor." Everyone seemed to say it at the same time.

"You are all very welcome. I'll send a nurse out when Alex is ready and you can go in. He's sedated and probably won't know you're there. But it will be good for you guys to see him. I'll check in with you tomorrow morning. Try and get some rest."

Everyone shook hands and the doctor departed, leaving each to their own thoughts to thank God for returning their precious son and brother to them.

Courtney had a difficult time focusing her attention on anything other than Alex's recovery. Her thoughts kept drifting back to another time, another place, back to 2002, when she nearly lost her mother through the incompetence of a surgeon. And she vowed that would not happen to her son. Not on her watch.

"David, I'm spending the night in Alex's room. I don't want him being alone." Courtney announced to David and Cameron.

Knowing better than to try and talk her out of it, David agreed. "It's probably a good idea in light of what happened to your mother. After we see Alex, I'll take Cam back to the hotel with me for the night."

"That's a good idea." Courtney said.

Their attention became diverted from their thoughts when the door opened and a nurse entered the room.

"You may go in now. He's still sedated, but he's resting comfortably." The nurse said.

"The doctor said I could spend the night in his room." Courtney blurted out just making sure the nurse got the message.

"Yes, Ma'am. We've been told by the doctor. Now would you like to follow me?" She said as she led the way.

"Thank you." Courtney said, as she led her family behind the nurse to Alex's room.

Holding Alex's hand, tears of relief flooded Courtney's eyes. They all stood quietly looking down at the boy in the bed. Knowing no matter what his age, he'll always be their little boy. He lay there silently breathing, while tubes and wires and machines making strange sounds, pervaded their space while doing their part in his recovery. The worst was over. Now it was time to get Alex on the road to recovery.

After David and Cameron left to go to their hotel, Courtney called her parents again.

"Hello." Carroll said reaching for the phone as Art yelled for her to put it on speaker.

"Hi. We just left Alex in recovery. He looked so small in that bed. It reminded me of when he was born and was in the incubator for so long. Oh, how we all worried. And, here I go again, standing over my son's bed, looking at him hooked up to every contraption imaginable." The tears flowed from her eyes as her voice cracked with images of old memories.

"We know, honey. We know," Art and I said, holding back our own tears. The last thing she needed right now was for us to come apart. She needed our strength. Not our weakness.

"But he's going to be fine. The doctor was very reassuring. And he should know. You've been under so much tension since this all began last August your body is releasing all that pent up stress and worry. Just let it go. You have so much to be thankful for. Alex is strong and he's young. He's going to be alright and he's going to be free of pain and back to being our *old Alex* again. Okay?"

"I guess, Mom, but . . ."

"No buts. No more buts. Do you hear me? Just smiles and love. That's what he needs to see when he opens his eyes. Lots of smiling faces expressing tons of love. Trust me, that's the best medicine he can have," I said, so relieved, yet thinking that the mask we wear is often more rewarding than the face it hides.

"Hi, honey, I just got on too." Art said, as he listened to our conversation before joining in. "Mom and I are really happy to hear the good news. He'll be up, walking, and going home before you know it. I'm glad you're spending the night with him. You're a great little nurse, honey. You should be, you've certainly had enough practice with your mother."

"Thanks, Daddy. As soon as he's ready to be moved to his room, I'll go with him. I'll call you guys in the morning. Okay?"

"Sounds like a plan." Art said. "Goodnight, Hon."

"Goodnight, Daddy."

"Courtney," I said, before hanging up. "Try and get some sleep. But if you find you need to talk, call me and don't worry about the time. You know me. When that phone goes off, I'm wide awake. So call if you want to. Okay?"

"Thanks, Mom. Love you guys. Goodnight."

"Night, night, Honey." I said, hanging up.

"I'm so glad everything went well." I said, breathing a huge sigh of relief.

"Yeah, me too. And I'm really glad she's spending the night. We sure as hell don't need another fiasco," Art said, shaking his head. "I don't know about you, but I'm going to bed. It's been a long day and I'm pooped."

"I'll be there shortly. I think I'll watch television for a little while and unwind."

"Alright," Art said, making his way to the bedroom.

CHAPTER 36

Today is Thursday, March 29, and Alex has been up and walking since Tuesday morning.

Yesterday he had his first food, Jell-O and broth, not exactly what you might call gourmet dining, but it tasted really good to him, nevertheless.

They're going to remove his IV's and his pain pump today, thus administering his meds orally.

If all goes well today, he will go home to recuperate for a week before heading back to college.

This has been a long and painful journey for everyone involved. But no one was any more distressed than me. I knew what was in my grandson's head and his heart. I was especially saddened when Courtney told me the results of the pathology report. He does indeed have Crohn's disease. Even though I had already prepared myself for those results, I still didn't want to hear them.

I think I knew he had Crohn's before the doctors did. I knew this when he became so ill in November, 2011. My *Why* had finally been answered. It was now up to me to help Alex through tough times and to teach him how to help others with same disease.

God didn't give up on me those forty plus years ago, even though I had nearly given up on myself. I truly believe that when He sees someone who refuses to quit, no matter the obstacles, He looks down from above and says, "Now there's someone I can use." He has chosen me, even at my age, to help others who are having difficulty adjusting to a horrible, incurable disease. There is only one decision we can make that can keep us from reaching God's goals in our lives, and that is to *QUIT.* It's the only way to lose. And for me quitting is not an option.

Forty years ago when God spoke to me that cold Minnesota Thursday in March at Mayo Clinic, I heard Him. I listened to His words. But

I don't think I was prepared to thoroughly understand what He was saying to me.

Looking back upon those forty years, there were times, many times, when I was encouraged to write about my Crohn's experience. But I wasn't ready. I was unable to see the forest for the trees. Like a ship without a rudder, drifting aimlessly on a sea of doubts, of why's. When my answer stood in front of my very eyes, I could not see it. I lacked direction, through my own fault, no one else's. I had lost my goal and my vision. In order to become excited about your work you must be excited about your goal.

The greatest limitations in one's life are self-imposed. In the words of John Ruskin, "The highest reward for man's toil is not what he gets for it, but what he becomes by it."

Think about that simple sentence. It's probably one of the most profound you'll ever hear. So if you remember nothing else, please remember that powerful little sentence.

At sometime or other in our lives, we'll all be forced to live through some kind of storm. Maybe for you it will be the end of a marriage, or perhaps the loss of a loved one. For me it was nearly losing my life. Not once, but twice. And the oddest thing about the two occasions is they both happened during the Easter Holy Week of both years. God was talking to me. I was listening, but I wasn't hearing. Another *Why* in my life already heaped with *Whys*.

Well, like it or not, sooner or later, adversity comes knocking on everyone's door. And it's times like this when we question whether life is worth living. Are my hopes and dreams really worth the price?

My answer to you is "absolutely." In times like these it's too easy to give up and give in. To quit. To make excuses why we aren't successful. If times weren't so tough, maybe I could get ahead. I just can't seem to win for losing.

I have a theory that if we take the problems of everyone we know and toss them into a great big box, shake them up, and select only those we think we might want, I'll bet you'd pick your own. If you look at all the problems of your friends, and not their successes, somehow you begin to see and appreciate yours in a whole new light. A brand new perspective.

Someone once said that "champions have no sense of blame." It's the one trait common to all great and unfailing champions . . . the absence of an attitude of not taking responsibility. Just ask any of our Olympians. I'll bet they'll tell you the same thing.

When others are at fault, they don't sulk or censure. When they are to blame, they never rage at themselves. In the heart of every great champion resides something called *temperament*, which is an inborn trait. A champion has an innate ability to ascertain whether someone is self-destroying or self-fulfilling. The difference between one champion and another may be minute in terms of endurance, but colossal in terms of heart. Champions are beyond tribute, beyond accountability. In the heat of battle, the champion forgets who he is and concentrates solely and passionately on that which is before him instinctively striving for perfection that quietly obliterates the man seeking it. Champions never beat themselves up – they merely forget themselves.

So step up to the plate and don't be afraid to take that first swing. Sure you may strike out, but I'll guarantee you that if you keep practicing, keep swinging, you'll not only hit a home run, but you'll knock the ball clean out of the ballpark.

CHAPTER 37

L earn to listen. Yes, you heard correctly! Listening is an art, one which most of the population has yet to learn, including me. I love to talk. That's not entirely a bad thing. But trust me, listening is so much better. Learning how to listen, for a talker like me, is a real challenge. I must admit, I'm still not a skilled listener, but I never stop trying. It demands a lot of effort, a lot of discipline, and most importantly, an unselfish attitude. Listening is an all-important tool for personal growth. Yet, it's one of the least developed skills people have. However, sadly as it is, most of us do far more talking than we do listening.

There's an old adage. "Man is born with two ears, but only one tongue. Which means we should listen twice as much as we talk?"

How many of you listen to music? I would venture to guess most everyone, certainly at one time or another, some on a daily basis, others occasionally. But, how often do you take the time to sit quietly and *listen* to the music? For me, it's a daily ritual. I listen and I hear. What's the difference, you ask? Hearing tells you that the music is playing. Listening tells you what the song is saying.

There are actually two different kinds of listening. There is natural listening while interacting with others. Then there is the spiritual type as we listen to the voice of God.

A good leader learns to monopolize the listening, not the talking. What we learn about someone else will always result in a much greater reward than what we tell him about ourselves.

Learn to not only listen, but aggressively observe and hear. *Really hear!*

The key to obtaining real success in this arena is to learn to listen to your conscience, to those around you who may be hurting either physically or mentally. And trust me, if someone is hurting physically I can almost guarantee he is hurting mentally.

Nowadays, there are so many who suffer in silence. I know this to be fact because I was one who suffered silently for years. Not wanting anyone to know of my illness, pride got in the way of good sense. So often, that's the case.

Learn to treat yourself first. The better you treat yourself, the better you'll be treated by others. As someone once said, it's time you sow good seeds in the soil of your own life and mind.

Amen to that, my friends.

Remember to surround yourself with good people. Positive people. People, who will build you up, not tear you down.

Paul Harvey once said, "If you want to get big fleas, hang out with big dogs."

So if you want to accomplish great things, I suggest you hang around great people, positive thinking people. Gordon Dean, former U.S. Atomic Commissioner Chairman, once said, "The way to become truly useful, is to seek the best that other brains have to offer. Use them to supplement your own, and give credit to them when they have helped."

Hold fast to your dream and don't allow it to slip away. Dreams have a way of disappearing when we least expect it. Ratchet up your courage and your attitude. Stop your belly-aching and complaining. It serves no purpose. Allow yourself to grow into greatness. The tiny acorn grows into a mighty oak as do the seeds of greatness within our own lives. But like the mighty oak, it takes time and nurturing and lots of patience.

Remember we never get a second chance to make a first impression. Be confident! Be knowledgeable. Knowledge breeds confidence. Know what you believe and why. And for heaven's sake, as well as your own, cut the umbilical cord to your past failures. Only carry forth the good decisions and victories of your past. The good seeds you sow today will determine what you harvest tomorrow.

Become a part of someone else's miracle, and it will come back to you in spades.

Learn how to tame your tongue. Yep! You heard correctly. Learn to tame that tongue of yours. This is one area that we all seem to be guilty of. Some of us more than others. It's the most powerful or destructive force in your life. Controlling your tongue means controlling your life. Your tongue alone can make or break someone. It can tear them down or build them up. The choice is yours. I suggest you choose wisely. Especially in this era of social media.

Remember, my friends, as the old saying goes, "you were not made to dig in the dirt with the chickens, but you were made to soar in the clouds with the wings of an eagle."

So stop scratching and start soaring. We're only on this earth for a short time and no matter how hard we try, none of us are getting out of it alive. When they back that hearse up to your front door, believe me, they're not making a trial run.

For Pete's sake, stop spending a dollar's worth of time for a dime's worth of results.

Many people spend entire lives in fields of endeavor or professions that have nothing to do with their God given, inborn talents. Learn to recognize your special talents and do everything you can to capitalize on them. By taking that one little step, that initiative, you're taking the master key given to you by God to open the door to opportunity in your life. So take advantage of it.

God's gifts are never loans; they are always deposits. But only you can determine the interest on them. Hence, they are never used up or depleted. In fact, the more they're used, the more valuable they become in providing the knowledge and wisdom which cannot be received any other way or by any other source. It is your responsibility to make good use of all the gifts He has given you.

Most people allow someone else to control their destiny. Don't let that happen to you. Your life is your vehicle and you are in the driver's seat. Let nothing hold you back. God's gifts are for you to use and to help those lives who are attached to those gifts. What I'm trying to tell you, is simply this, there are those whose lives will be directly affected by the gift God has bestowed upon you. So wake up and while you still can, help someone who's suffering.

Believe me when I tell you this. It took me more than forty years to realize what God had been trying to tell me. Once, when He whispered in my ear and next when He brought me back to life; and I was still too thick headed to realize I had a job to do. I didn't understand His message. I just . . . didn't get it. Or maybe I wasn't ready to understand it.

Chapter 38

It took my grandson's diagnosis of Crohn's disease for me to finally realize that I now knew the reason God had spared my life ... *twice!* This was His plan for me, His gift to me. It was now my turn to share His gift to help others in a way that only I knew how; my forty-plus years of expertise in managing life with an ileostomy and Crohn's disease. To be able to share my gift with my grandson, Alex, so he can, one day, share his gift with someone in need. Learning to teach someone how to live the rest of their life with a disease that is incurable is a real mission. It's manageable, yes. Curable ... *no.* But you can learn to manage it and manage it successfully. To live a full and happy life while in remission, doing everything you did before.

The true test of what we're made of comes when we fall out of remission. That's when you have to dig down deep within yourself and pull forth all the positive energy you can. And then with God's help and your friends and family, you'll discover what you are *really* made of. No guts - No glory!

You have to take care of those vulnerable times in your days, the first thing in the morning and the last thing at night. Someone once said, what a person is like at midnight when he is all alone reveals that person's true self. I firmly believe that.

Everyone has the same number of hours in a day. *Twenty-four.* No more. No less. Rich or poor, we're all the same. It's what we choose to do with our time that defines who we are. If you take control of your time, you'll take control of your life.

Don't be like the airline pilot flying over the Pacific Ocean who announces to his passengers, "Folks, I've got some good news and some bad. The bad news is we're lost. The good news, I'm happy to report, is we're making great time!"

Try to keep in mind that the future arrives an hour at a time. And it's no different for you or anyone else.

It's now time for you to get rid of that albatross that's been hanging around your neck for far too long. You know what I'm talking about. It's that thing you've been dragging about from your past. Don't think you're so special. You're not. You're just like the rest of us. At one time or another we've allowed our past to monopolize way too much of our time. For many of you, it still is; unless you do something about it, it will take hold and never let go for the rest of your life. It's so easy to get caught up in yourself, your own self pity and what you're having to deal with, that you forget about everyone else. You know what's wrong with you, so deal with it.

This may sound a little callous and to a degree, perhaps it is. I'm not one to sugarcoat things as important as one's health.

How do I know this? Well I have several friends who have been dragging something from their past around with them all their lives. Until they make a concerted effort to rid themselves of it, it'll eat them alive. And it is.

There's one case in particular where this very thing has happened. No matter how many times she tells me that it really doesn't make that much difference, to her it makes a lot of difference. So much so that she can't stop talking about it. It's eating her alive. My prayer for my friend is that she cut the worst of her past loose and let go of it. It does nothing but drag her down. I see it on her face and in her eyes each time she talks about it. She's much too fine a person to allow the past to strangle her future.

After a while, people become disenchanted with the same old war stories about your illness. It's a reminder they'd soon forget. You have it, they know it, and would just as soon forget it. When someone asks you how you are? Please answer by saying, "I'm doing just great, thanks for asking." No one really wants to hear how you're *really* feeling. Trust me on this.

The more we look backward, the less able we are to see forward. Failure is always lurking just around some corner for those of you who are reveling in yesterday's successes and failures. Choose to be forward-focused and not past-possessed.

How many times have you heard the phrase, there's nothing to fear but fear itself. Well, my friends, here's something to chew on: *Fear and worry are interest paid in advance on something you may never own.* Think about it carefully. We've all been, at one time or another, part and parcel to this very thing. Worry is simply the triumph of fear over faith.

Someone once said, fear is a poor chisel to carve out tomorrow. It strangles and chokes off the creative flow from above. Things are rarely what they seem. You can dwell on or worry about things that are beyond your control 'til you're blue in the face and the only thing you will really accomplish is negativity. Please don't get me wrong, I'm not telling you that you'll never worry about this disease, you'll always worry in some way or other. Just look how much I worry about Alex. It's a normal response in our brain. But, you can't allow it to control your life.

You've got to learn to set goals. How many of you have a goal? We all need goals. Mine, for now, is to make it my mission for the rest of my life to see that *you* have the help you need to manage your disease. The first thing you'll need to do that is a roadmap.

Hopefully, everything I've been sharing with you will somehow get you to think about where you are headed in your life. What direction you need to take in order to get you there. My expectations with this book are to at least get you started on the right road, headed in the right direction. If I'm successful in doing that, then I've accomplished something great.

Think of your goal as a dream with a deadline. First, you have to define your goal (dream). Then write it down. That's the power of the dream. Putting it on paper. Once you have committed your goal in writing, you have taken that first big step toward achievement. Now, run with it; don't walk. Walking will only tempt you to venture off in the opposite direction. By running fast with your vision in sight, it's next to impossible to get lost, turn around and head back.

And during this trip of yours, the lessons you'll learn along the way will be of greater importance to you than achieving the goal itself.

I know this first-hand because as I began telling others that I was writing a book about Crohn's, IBD's, and ostomies, I've had so many people tell me that they either have a friend or family member who is suffering from this disease and having a book such as this at their disposal, will be enormously helpful. Having people thank me for something I'd yet finished was all it took for me to realize that not only have I defined my own dream, but I might just possibly help others to define theirs.

So although this positive thinking stuff you are now reading may seem a little out of whack, somewhere out in left field, I assure you it is exactly where it should be. Right in front of you, for you to read and read and read, until you finally get it through your head that it is precisely what you need to be hearing and at a time you *definitely* need to hear it.

CHAPTER 39

Remember what I told you about listening and hearing. Well I encourage you to read this with an open mind and listen to the words, and really hear what they are telling you. If it takes you a hundred times of reading it for you to actually get it, then I suggest you do whatever it takes to reach your goal. I think you'll surprise yourself.

I told you earlier in my story how long it took me to realize that God had a plan for me, yet I was too lost to realize it. Too bad I didn't have a book like this to help get my head in the right place. To help me realize how much I was hurting myself by *not* understanding what was in front of me.

Don't be like me. Be wise enough to be on the lookout for unexpected and exciting new paths on your journey. Columbus discovered America while searching for a route to India. They might call that dumb luck. Maybe, but I think he was destined to find America. And, I'm so glad he didn't give up *his* journey.

Be happy. *You Are Alive!* That in itself is worth celebrating. But you must make a conscious effort to smile. Smiling is a choice and not a result.

Helen Keller once said, "Keep your face to the sunshine and you cannot see the shadow."

Great advice, I'd say, wouldn't you? Don't you think it's about time to get out of the shadows and into the sunlight? The bigger your problems or challenges, the more you need to smile. Our attitude is like a barometer. It tells others what we expect in return. As your enthusiasm increases, you'll find your fears and stress levels will decrease. Being happy is like a cold—it's extremely contagious.

No one has ever accomplished greatness without enthusiasm. Remember that! You too can achieve whatever degree of greatness you desire. It is up to you. Just remember not to quit once you have been victorious. The greatest prize of victory is the opportunity to do more.

Learn to be the snowball, not the snowman. "What in the world is she talking about, now?" you may be asking yourself. Well here's your answer. How many times have you built a snowman? For most of you, the answer will probably be, many. But for those of you who have never seen snow, you'll just have to roll along with what I'm about to tell you.

A snowman stands there looking great, but serves no purpose. That's about the extent of his role. Like a lot of us, as we go about our lives with no real purpose. We just stand around looking great. That's about it, right?

Not the snowball, however. He's a real achiever. He doesn't just stand about doing nothing. He can do many things, including becoming a snowman. You start your tiny snowball at the top of the hill; give it a push, and watch out below. Its momentum will not only pick up steam, but by the time it reaches the bottom it has grown to enormous proportions. It didn't stop along the way. It didn't take a detour. It didn't question its potential. Nope, it just kept rolling and rolling and getting bigger and bigger. There's no way to pick up your tiny snowball, now.

Think of that rolling snowball as your goal. It started small and by persisting it grew larger and larger. Now it's so big that it enables you to not only enjoy your accomplishment in its growth, but it enables you to share your good fortune with someone else by helping them to build their own rolling snowball. Get the picture?

It's high time to let go of whatever is holding you back. Please try and remember this: "What is *in* you will always be bigger than whatever is *around* you."

Never be afraid to fail. Only those who never try, never fail. It is always better to fail at doing something, than to succeed in doing nothing. Those who have no failures, also, have very few victories. The choice is up to us. We can elect to turn our failures into a hitching post, or a guidepost.

I don't know about you, but I'm through with hitching posts. I would much prefer using my failures as a great learning experience. "Learn the lessen. Forget the details." That is my motto.

I can assure you I've had to learn a myriad of lessons in my lifetime. I can almost guarantee that I'll have a heck of a lot more left to learn before I hang up my Gucci pumps.

Every great thing ever accomplished was made by someone whose faith ran ahead of their minds. Most of us will spend entire lives lowering our buckets into empty wells. We'll while away our days bringing them back up time after time as empty as they went into that well.

Isn't it about time for you to drill a new well?

Concentrate on the important things in life, not the unimportant. "If you are hunting rabbits in tiger country, you must keep your eye peeled for tigers. But, when you're hunting tigers, you can ignore the rabbits." I love this jewel by H. Stern.

Forget the rabbits in you life and just concentrate on hunting the big game. Dream big.

God knows you're worth it and so do I.

Surround yourself with the right people. Those who bring out the best in you. It's far better to be alone than in the wrong company. Just one conversation with the right person can prove to be far more valuable than all your years of learning. I don't care how many degrees you might have.

I have been very fortunate to have met many people in my life who have influenced me in positive ways. Those who possessed great faith in themselves and in God. They saw the potential in me when I failed to realize it in myself.

I have made many positive changes in my life. I also learned that keeping positive is an ongoing chore. But, believing in yourself is the secret ingredient. Dare to be great!! You can be.

CHAPTER 40

I think the greatest compliment that anyone will ever give you is to say that you are *different*. Strive to be different. To make necessary changes in your life. Strive to stand out, not blend in. If there is nothing *in* your life, perhaps it's time to re-evaluate your life.

Learn to do the ordinary things in life in extraordinary ways. Don't be intimidated one way or the other by group opinion. It makes no difference whether anyone else believes. Only *you* must believe. In fact, the two worst things you can say to yourself when you have an idea are, (1) It's *never* been done before. Or (2) It *has* been done before. Just because someone else has gone a particular route doesn't mean that you, too, will fail. How many times have you watched a gas station of the corner have owner after owner open it, only to close it yet again. They couldn't make a go of it. Until one day, along comes someone else who takes the same failure of a gas station, opens it and makes it a huge success. It happens everyday.

Be a pioneer. Blaze your own trail; learn to stand out. And don't be afraid to say *no*. It can be a powerful word. It can turn a situation from bad to good. From wrong to right. From ugly to exquisite. It holds the ability in those two simple letters – n and o – to lift many of the burdens you may now be facing. You simply cannot be all things to all people all the time. Your life's destiny is determined by these two simple words. Saying "no" to simpler less important things, can mean saying "yes" to the more significant things in life.

Why are we so afraid of making changes in our lives? Changing need not be the direct opposite of what or who you are now. It may be merely an adjustment or an addition in your life. Like it or not, you will at one time or another, be forced to make changes. So be prepared. People have been custom-built for change. Think about it, we have been changing continually from birth. And we didn't even realize it, did we? The more we change, the more we grow.

Take a chance and be willing to make positive changes in your life.

You are a leader. Learn to accept that responsibility and be the best you can be. Have no regrets. An old proverb says "An army of sheep led by a lion would defeat an army of lions led by a sheep." I know which I strive to be. Do you? We were all born originals. But sadly, most die copies.

My prayer for you is not to be a copy. You're one of a kind. Don't ever cheat yourself and be less than what you were made to be. The measure of a man is not what he does on Sunday, but rather who he is on Monday through Saturday. God will use you right where you happen to be today. Right now! Right here! You don't have to do anything spiritually special. Be anything or anyone special. He uses people from all walks of life. Heck, just look at me. I'm not anyone special or prominent. I'm just me. Just . . . *Carroll*

God spoke to me in a very uplifting and particular way. I wasn't in a church. I wasn't even praying at the time. I was feeling sorry for myself lying in my hospital bed with my television going, crying about what was going to happen to me, and I was all alone.

But, He had something special in mind for me. A plan. I listened to His words that day, but I didn't hear His message. It took me more than forty years to hear what He was trying to tell me. Or did it? Maybe that was God's plan for me all along. To stumble through the dark until I was ready to see the light. I guess I'll never really know the answers to those questions. It really doesn't matter when I realized what I was meant to do, only that I did realize it and I was prepared to hear God's message to me.

CHAPTER 41

I know now what I was destined to do with my life. The lessons I've learned along the way these past seventy-six plus years, have all been in preparation for what I am doing this very moment. Writing down the trials and tribulations of the past forty years. My triumphs and my tragedies.

My hopes and prayers for you are that perhaps you will take something from this book to help you through some challenging times in your life. If but only one person garners a simple passage or maybe only a single word from my story, then I will have accomplished what I set out to do.

You are a winner. I know that and you know that deep down. It has probably been buried in some dark corner of your mind. It's high time to dig deep and bring your winning spirit forth.

You'll never know what great things are out there just waiting for you to seize them. You deserve to live a fulfilling life. So live it.

My final advice to you shall be this. Have hope. Have faith. Be the person God meant for you to be. Don't settle for anything less. Don't look back. Only look ahead and move one step at a time in the direction God has laid out for you.

If God is for us, who cares who's against us, that's my new motto. You see, God had a plan for me, and dying wasn't it. I still have a lot of work to do. And with His help and guidance, I'll complete my journey. And so will you.

I hope I have given you the answers to some of your questions regarding Crohn's disease, IBD's and ostomies. I hope along the route you have given me the opportunity to lead you into a positive frame of mind. Life is so full of negativity that a little positive remark sometimes can help to heal a lot of open wounds. I know because I allowed my wounds to fester for far too long and look where it got me. Nowhere, until I was forced to see the light and hear the answer to my question. *WHY?*

CHAPTER 42

As I live each day in reflection of what was then and what is to-day, I find I'm living in a parallel world which alternates between steep highs and sharp lows. Learning conflicted terms as grief, guilt, and pride. I experienced all of these as I wrote my book. I shed copious tears as I typed the words on these pages. I learned from each the importance they played in my life. I would not be the person I am today had it not been for the lessens learned along the way.

My journey is far from over. It is however, nearer the end than the beginning. I'm not at all fazed by that knowledge. It's life and life happens. There is a beginning, a middle, and an end. No matter how hard you try, or how rich you are, it's the one thing we all have in common. There's not a damn thing we can do to stop the natural progression.

See to it that you keep the minor things of life . . . minor. And in the process, make sure you keep the major ones . . . major.

For those of you who have made my life worth living, my family, my friends, please don't question yourselves after I'm gone if there was something more you could have done to have kept me one more hour. One more day. I will tell you all ahead of time, and we will not speak of it again. You gave your all and so much more, to ensure my life would be better than it was. Trust me; your best was indeed good enough. It was better than good enough. It was stupendous. Glorious. Something that defies explanation. You were the best of the best. Just know that you have, indeed, given your all, and that's about all anyone can do.

I was so fortunate in having had the luxury of calling you my friend, my dear precious family. I don't wish to sound morose. That's not what I'm about. I only hope you will get on with your lives allowing them to unfold with grace and ease. Live them to the fullest giving of your-selves in positive meaningful ways. God will reward you in more ways than you can possibly imagine. And I shall always be there for you. If only in your heart. When you need me, all you have to do is call my name and feel my presence. I shall be there . . . *Just look up.*

    May God bless you all.
        Your friend, Carroll.....

P.S. Remember when I told you that Holy Week seemed to play an important part in my episodes both at Mayo Clinic in 1971, and again in Sarasota in 2002. Well, it happened once more. I finished handwriting my manuscript of Palm Sunday, this year, 2012. The day before Alex was released from the hospital after recuperating from surgery. Yes, his stay in the hospital was also during Holy Week.

    Yeah, I know. It gave me Goosebumps, too. I have no answers to why those events happened during that time. Again, another *WHY*, in my life which seems to be plagued with them.

EPILOGUE TO ALEXANDER deCARLE WEST

Yes, the day my *why* was answered was a bittersweet one for me. But it was a day that turned my life around. A day that will forever live in infamy in my mind and my heart.

I am working on a daily basis to eradicate those terrible feelings of guilt I've been harboring since I learned of Alexander's Crohn's disease. That is not quite the legacy I had hoped to leave to my grandson. But it is, nevertheless, the one I have been obliged to leave.

It's normal to feel guilty. But it's also normal to learn to let go of your guilt. There's nothing you can do about it that you haven't already done. All I can be is the best me I know how to be. In the process, hopefully have Alex see that he, too, can be the best person he can be. To let him know that his grandmother is the biggest cheerleader in his camp. That I would walk through fire if I knew I could change his diagnosis Take away his Crohn's disease. I wish I could be at his side every moment he needed me. I can't do that, and I'm sure he wouldn't want me to. Just having you in my life, Alex, has blessed me in so many ways. God created this very special relationship between us. I've been so fortunate to have played a small part in the man you have become. It engulfs my heart with tremendous pride, knowing that you take my heart with you everywhere you choose to go.

You bring the sunshine after the rain. Your smile contains a magic that erases all doubts.

Your love fills my empty places. I will love you unconditionally until the day I die and beyond. That is a promise I know I can keep, my precious grandson. I love you, Alex. No matter what. You shall forever be special.

Your life stands tall on the threshold of many great tomorrows. There are so many things you will accomplish in your lifetime. So many things I wish for you. But, while on your life's journey, keep forever in your heart my seven important principles: Faith, Love, Courage, Honesty, Compassion, Humility, and Forgiveness.

We all make mistakes in life, Alex, but the true measure of a great man is his ability to forgive. Forgiveness may be the hardest thing you'll ever have to do. No good comes from harboring anger, rage, or bitterness. They're like open wounds that will fester and if left untreated only get worse. So please learn to forgive. It is a choice that comes with a price . . . *risk*. The risk of acceptance or rejection. Bear in mind, the first person forgiveness changes is the one doing the forgiving.

Like anything else we attempt, it comes with uncertainty. We have no idea how it will be accepted. However, you took the first step and that's a huge start. You have extended the gauntlet. It's now up to the other person to either pick it up or simply walk away. The onus is theirs, just as it was yours to proffer the choice. You did your job. You forgave. Rest assured, my grandson, it will lift you beyond your greatest expectations. Believe in yourself and don't hesitate to take God's hand and allow him to lead you down the right path. He'll *never* steer you wrong.

My greatest wish for you, long after I have departed this earth, is to learn to cope with your disease and no matter what you are compelled to face in the future regarding your Crohn's, I pray you will pick up this book and re-read it and use your life's experiences, as well as mine, to enhance the lives of others who may not have had the benefit of a family member to supply them with a host of wisdom. Wisdom achieved through much trial and error. Remember always, that above those darkened clouds the sun shines forever bright.

Through time, I hope you will discover that your greatest strengths lie in your weaknesses. Through all of this, please know how much I love you. Far more than words can say. You, my wonderful grandson, are a very precious part of me.

No matter where your travels take you, Alex, my love is with you always,

Nana

Resources

ORGANIZATIONS

There are chapters of the Crohn's and Colitis Foundation and the United Ostomy Association throughout the United States, Canada, and most of the world. Check your telephone directory or the internet for a chapter near you and please join.

United States

Crohn's and Colitis Foundation of America
733 Third Avenue, Suite 510
New York, New York 10017
(800) 932-2423
(888) 694-8872 to speak to a specialist
Email address: info@ccfa.org
Website: www.ccfa.org

United Ostomy Association of America
P.O. Box 525
Kennebunk, ME 04043-0525
(800) 826-0826
Email address: info@uoaa.org
Website: www.uoaa.org
Affiliated support groups

International Ostomy Association
www.ostomyinternational.org

IDEAS for Kids (Intestinal Disease Education & Awareness Society)
1859 Napier St.
Vancouver BC V5L 2N4, Canada
1-604-255-9606
Website: www.ideaskids.com
Website: www.weneedideas.ca
Email: info@ideas-na.com

Young Ostomate & Diversion Alliance of America
Website: www.yodaa.org (Ages 18 through 3
1052 NE 102nd Street - Seattle, WA 98124

Pull-thru Network
1705 Wintergreen Parkway
Normal, IL 61761
309-262-0786
Website: www.pullthrunetwork.org
Email: pullthrunetwork@gmail.com
(Information & support for children & parents)

Shadow Buddies
1-913-642-4646
Website: www.shadowbuddies.org
Email: buddies@shadowbuddies.org
(Dolls with ostomies)

Gay and Lesbian Ostomates
1-773-286-4005
Website: www.abiggerlife.com

Osto Group
Website: www.ostogroup.org
(Free ostomy supplies for those in the USA without Medicare or other health
insurance; postage & small handling cost)

American Cancer Society
Website: www.cancer.org
(800) ACS-2345

Canada

Crohn's and Colitis Foundation of Canada
600-60 St. Clair Avenue E.
Toronto, Canada M4T 1N5
(416) 920-5035
(800) 387-1479
Email address: support@crohnsandcolitis.ca
Website: www.crohnsandcolitis.ca

United Ostomy Association of Canada, Inc.
5800 Ambler Drive Suite 210.
Mississauga, ON L4W 4J4 Canada
(905-212-7111)
(888) 969-9698 (within Canada)
Email address: info1@ostomycanada.ca
Website   : www.ostomycanada.ca

Canada Cancer Society National Office
55 St. Clair Ave., West Suite 300
Toronto, Ontario M4V M4V 2Y7 Canada
Website: www.cancer.ca
Email: connect@cancer.ca

International

International Ostomy Association
Website: www.ostomyinternational.org

International IBD (International Bowel Disease) Association
Email: http://ibdcrohns.about.com

Asia and South Pacific Ostomy Association
www.ostomyasiasouthpacific.org

Books

Crohn's Disease & Ulcerative Colitis by Fred Saibil, MD
IBD Self-Management (The AGA Guide to Crohn's Disease and Ulcerative Colitis) by Sunanda V. Kane, MD, MSPH

The Ostomy Book by Barbara Dorr Mullen & Kerry Anne McGinn, RN, ARNP (Third Edition – Revised & Updated)

This is just a small compilation of the books that are available on the internet or your bookstores. If you are interested in which celebrities such as athletes, singers, dancers, etc., you'll find quite a few. You see, this insidious disease can affect *anyone*. And it does.

INTIMACY FOR MEN AND WOMEN

SPECIAL SECTION DEVOTED ENTIRELY TO ADULT PATIENTS WITH ILEOSTOMIES, COLOSTOMIES OR UROSTOMIES

This is perhaps the most important chapter in my book mainly because it deals with things that people are so reluctant to speak openly about. It's as though they don't exist when in fact without sound advice, it's the one thing that could quite possibly either make or break a relationship with your partner or future partner.

Intimacy! It's nearly a taboo word. Sad, but true. Like it or not, I feel compelled to offer some advice that has helped save me from possibly ruining my own intimate relationship with my husband. Hopefully, it will help some of you as well.

After I had finished writing my book, my husband, Art, asked me if I had covered intimacy and its importance in a relationship. My answer was, "I don't think so; at least not to any significant degree."

"Well don't you think it warrants at least its own special chapter? After all, we certainly had our ups and downs throughout our forty-seven year marriage. Especially in the beginning when there was no help from anyone willing to share their knowledge of intimacy with us. We basically had to figure out everything on our own. What to wear during those intimate moments. Boy, that was interesting. Remember?"

"Oh, do I. We had to invent our own sexy underwear for me to wear and that was hysterical. I ended up going to Wal-Mart and purchasing those puckered tube tops that women wore back forty plus years ago. We than used them to go around my tummy to hold my pouch from coming off or flapping about during sex. When I think of those times now, I really have to laugh. We didn't know if I should step into it and pull it up or put it over my head and pull it down to my tummy. God, we must have been a sketch."

"Yeah," Art said. "But had it not been for my ingenious idea to use to those dumb tube tops, God knows what we would have come up with. It's a good thing we didn't think to film it. No one would have believed the antics or gymnastics we were forced to go through just to make that damn pouch look like anything but a *damn pouch.*"

Art and I couldn't stop laughing at all the years of things we had to attempt from making our own crotchless panties and pantyhose to our fancy pouch covers and pouch bibs.

Yes, Art was the man who was directly affected by my illness from the beginning to the present. He guided us through treacherous and turbulent times in our lives and was always there to help steer me through the most intimate moments of our lives. Had it not been for his strength, belief, patience and love during those harrowing times, I don't know where I'd be. He literally forced me to look within myself to see the person I really was. That I hadn't changed just because I had this pouch on my tummy. I was still that girl he'd fallen in love with so long ago and had blessed him with two beautiful children. He refused to give up on us and he would not allow me to give up either. He kept reminding me that I had always been a strong woman and there was no reason to be anything but, especially now, when I needed to believe how strong I really was. This was not the time to be timid or weak about myself. This was the time to dig in and go forward with my life. I had so much to live for and so much to give. Thank goodness for Art's insistence that our bedroom life after my ostomy surgery, continue as it had before everything spiraled out of control. That's what it took for me to realize that nothing had changed except for the pouch permanently attached to my abdomen.

"You're still one hell of a sexy woman, Carroll deCarle. I can see it and now it's about time you start believing that you *are* sexy. For you, it's more emotional than physical at this point. Big deal! So you have to wear a pouch. For God's sake, woman, you are *alive!* Yes, alive! Think about it Carroll. God sent you back to us. He didn't give up on you, so what gives you the right to give up on yourself? Can you honestly answer that? Tell me and our children that you are a quitter."

I lay there stunned by what my husband had just said and how strongly he'd said it. Art was right. He knew it and he knew I knew it. No, I was anything but a quitter. So why was I so afraid of my bedroom . . . Our bedroom? I didn't know.

"No, Art, I'm not a quitter. And I'm thankful that you aren't either. Why you're still here is both a mystery and a blessing. You've never let me down. I know at times, it's taken every ounce of strength not to give up on me. If you'll teach me how to be sexy again, I promise I'll really try. Where do we start?"

He smiled and with tears in his eyes he kissed me and held me tightly. When he pulled apart, he took me by my shoulders and looked deep into my eyes and said, "We start at the beginning. We learn to relax and enjoy the experience of sex as if we are beginners. Just two new lovers. And, in a sense, we are just that . . . beginners and new lovers. This is a new journey for us both. The paths are the same; we simply have to learn how to navigate them a little differently. That's all. And for me, navigation is not a problem. As a former Navy pilot, I learned to navigate across the Pacific by the stars and a sextant, and now as an airline captain, I'd say I'm pretty damn good at navigating through all sorts of turbulence. So this, my sexy beautiful wife, will be a walk in the park. You just leave it all up to me, okay?"

"Okay," I said, smiling through my tears. "What's first?"

"First, we get our heads screwed on straight. This means we get you an attitude check-up."

"What do you mean?" I said, already putting up barriers. "My attitude is just fine."

"Really, Carroll? Sorry to have to break the news to you, but your attitude, as of late, stinks."

"But . . ." I began to object and was stopped dead in my tracks.

"No buts. We wouldn't be having this discussion if your attitude were okay. We all need attitude adjustments from time to time. That's what makes us stronger and better people. Just knowing that we aren't perfect, yet striving to become better is the first step in healing both mind and body. Your attitude and how you view yourself will set the tone for how others view and treat you. If you grow comfortable in your new skin, your new body, I'll grow more comfortable as well. You'll teach all of us something only *you*, the patient, can possibly understand. Just remember to let us know or let me know when I do not understand your feelings. I don't have a crystal ball embedded in my forehead, so I can't read minds. And I really want to do everything I can to assure we have a great healthy relationship both in and out of the bedroom. Okay?"

"Okay. I can do that."

"Good girl. Now let's see how we can make your bag and your underwear a little sexier. I've got some ideas."

"Why does that not surprise me?" I said, laughing. "You've always been the idea man in this family. Thank God for that." We hugged, kissed and laughed like two giddy kids.

In time, I began to think of my ostomy as simply outdoor plumbing. "You have indoor plumbing and I have outdoor," I would say to Art, as we laughed. "You have to go when nature calls. I, on the other hand, choose when to visit the loo."

"Yeah, yeah, yeah," Art said. "Just don't forget who designed those sexy pouch covers when you're in the loo."

"How could I possibly. They are forever with me, reminding me of just how lucky I am to have a husband who's always thinking of ways to make me feel every inch a woman. How special you are and I love you so much Arthur MacDonald deCarle. So very much." I reached over and grabbed him and held on. We embraced, kissed and snuggled.

"I just thought of something besides the phrase *outdoor plumbing*." Art said.

"And what, pray tell, might that be?" I asked, pinching his love handle.

"Instead of calling your appliance outdoor plumbing, let's call it Harvey."

"Harvey? Who in hell is Harvey?" I asked, as I leaned up on one elbow, staring at Art, bewildered.

"You remember the Pulitzer Prize winning play written by Mary Chase about the invisible rabbit named Harvey? It began its long running play on Broadway in 1944, I think."

"I remember. There was also a movie with Jimmy Stewart. I saw that several times." I said smiling.

"Yeah, me too. So we now have a new name for your appliance. We'll simply call it, Harvey. How does that sound?"

"It sounds just fine my brainstorming husband. Now, why don't we put Harvey to sleep while we do the same?" I said, snuggling close to Art.

This was the beginning of my sexy new outlook on my new life with Harvey. I owe my entire positive outlook to two men in my life. Two powerfully brilliant and humble men. My husband, Art, and my savior, my Lord Jesus Christ; with whom all things are possible. Both men have taken my hand and led me on my exciting new journey. I've been forced to face some very severe challenges along life's paths, but, neither man has let me down; nor have they let go of my hand.

I've learned that sex isn't solely what happens between our legs, but more importantly, what happens between our ears. Everyone experiences sexual difficulties at one time or another during their lifetime. Sometimes they're emotional. Sometimes they're physical. Oftentimes, they may be both. And you needn't have an ostomy to be affected by them. How we think of ourselves, (that's the between the ears part) is that person we see when we look into the mirror and wonder how others see us, how they see our body. What happens between our legs is largely predicated on that thing that happens between our ears. That self-esteem part is threatened when we have an ostomy, as well as our feelings of sexuality. If allowed to fester, these challenges will become monumental.

Having a normal, healthy sexual lifestyle is a huge step for your self-esteem. I know this firsthand. I was so fortunate in having a man who would not allow me to quit being a woman. But, like everything in life, it came with a price. A small price in my case, but nevertheless . . . a price. Communication! Yes, plain old talking. Sounds so simple, yet it's one of the hardest things on earth for people to accomplish. The ability of mastering the art of communication is colossal. However, if you have any hope of strengthening your intimate relationship with your partner, you'd better learn to talk.

Most people are clueless regarding ostomy surgery and that's understandable. They've probably never heard of it or even know of anyone who's had it. They have no idea what a stoma looks like, how it's attached to the abdomen, how it works and how it affects your ability to have or not to have sex. You'll need to decide when, where and just how much to tell them. Just how much to share. If it's someone you are interested in having a future relationship with sexually, or if it is your partner, just don't elect to tell them when you're in the throws of passion and heat.

Not good timing.

All partners of ostomy patients suffer with many of the same maladies as the patient himself. That's why it's so important for you to discuss the things you anticipate they're feeling and attempting to deal with. Is your partner concerned about hurting you or your stoma? If not adequately explained, you might find yourself misinterpreting this as a rejection. Open communication is paramount for a good healthy and secure relationship. It is crucial they fully understand about two of the most personal of bodily functions . . . bodily elimination and sex. They'll take their cue from you. It's imperative that you realize your partner's feelings are real and shouldn't be dismissed any more than your own. *Now, please read this sentence again. It's important that you fully understand its meaning and implication.*

Quite possibly, the most important ingredient for a happy and healthy sex life is your attitude. It's up to you to do whatever it takes to ensure you feel free, relaxed and completely at ease with your body. And to do this you'll need to talk to your partner openly about the following list of issues.

- Any physical limitations (vaginal dryness or problems with erections)
- Persistent pain
- What sexual activities you're *not* comfortable with
- What sexual activities you *are* comfortable with
- Your mutual expectations
- Any apprehension or fears of nakedness, leakage, odors, being unlovable or rejected

All emotions which might impede or interfere with your desire to share sex, such as: guilt, resentment, anger, fear.

The more information you're willing to disclose, the fewer difficulties you'll have sharing your body. Talking about these issues is a giant leap forward to a healthy relationship.

I've put together a selection of important must-knows to help you feel more comfortable and sexy in the bedroom for both men and women.

- First and foremost, always practice *Safe Sex.* Use foams, lubricated condoms and other principles of contraception.
- Focus! Focus! Focus, on your beautiful experience, not your damn pouch.
- Be sure to empty your pouch before you begin, securing it properly with tape around the edges.
- Be certain to shower or bathe before beginning. To make it a little more exciting, try showering together.
- Wear something sexy to hide your pouch such as lacey crotchless panties. For men, over-sized silky boxers work fine.

- If all else fails, simply use your imagination and see what inspires you. That's what we did.

At the end of this chapter, please note a list of websites for you to visit to see what types of intimate undergarments are available for both men and women. I think you'll be pleasantly surprised. Also check out the list of medications for controlling gas and odor.

HINTS FOR WOMEN

- For vaginal dryness, use Astroglide, K-Y Jelly, or the new Intense, by K-Y. There are others I've seen in the pharmacy for the same purpose. But you have to try different ones to see which works best for you.
- Talk to your doctor about vaginal suppositories or hormone creams.
- Try crotchless panties, short nighties or crotchless or snap closure 'teddies.'
- If you don't successfully reach orgasm your first time or so after surgery, don't fret. It's absolutely normal.
- Some of the information in the men's section applies to women as well. Please do read it and extract from it what best suits you.

HINTS FOR MEN

- Consider wearing your cummerbund, if you have one, over your stoma/pouch to prevent the pouch from flopping about.
- Consider cool, sexy silk boxers to hide your pouch.
- Go to Victoria's Secret or their catalog and purchase several tube tops of spandex in dark sexy colors and step into it pulling it up until it covers your pouch. This is actually a great idea for both men and women. I know because I discovered it years ago and still use the tube tops.

What I'm about to tell you is probably the very best suggestion for both men and women to follow: and that is *laughter*. Learn to keep things positive and happy in the bedroom. Sex and surgery are not easy to laugh about. They're very serious. All the more reason to keep things upbeat and fun. Develop a sense of humor about it. Make up funny names for your stoma/pouch just as we did by calling mine, Harvey.

Trust me, laughter and fun are easily available and very adaptable to most any situation. They'll bring great comfort into your relationship. *Bathroom humor* is something that makes most people laugh. Use it to your advantage. You'll quickly quell those little embarrassing moments that always seem to present themselves at the most inopportune times in the life of an ostomy patient. Ease those moments with a little humor. Learn to laugh. It will serve you well.

I leave you with one more piece of advice. Please don't make your ostomy your chastity belt. Keep in mind – you can control it or it can control you.

Relationships are like waves. One minute you can be riding the crest of the wave and another time you find yourself beneath it struggling to stay afloat. It's up to you to keep the joy of sex alive. But sex alone doesn't keep your relationship strong, secure and vibrant. No, there are other things to help in that department. Simple things like the act of holding hands, hugging, cuddling, kissing and the art of stimulation by touch. If you feel good about yourself and your new body, your partner will very likely feel the same way. How we feel affects what we're able to do. Usually after surgery, it's often difficult to begin feeling *sexy* again. It's quite possible that you'll not have any sexual feeling for days, weeks, or even months. There's no need to worry, this is normal. How could you possibly even think about sex if you're still in pain or physically exhausted. You've got to allow you body sufficient time to recover and in doing so, learn to manage your stoma before even considering any strenuous intimacies in the bedroom.

The first time you become intimate after surgery, don't be disappointed if things don't go as you planned. Men may have difficulty getting or keeping an erection. Women often experience pain or vaginal dryness during intercourse. It's easy to convince yourself that your surgery has ruined your sex life forever. But think about it? Is the real culprit the surgery? Perhaps it's your own worries and fears in your ability to perform. Will your stoma or your pouch offend your partner? Will it leak or fall off or have a foul odor? Do you feel unattractive or depressed? Are your medications interfering with your sexuality? Or, maybe you're simply not strong enough. You can't blame your ostomy for all your problems or feelings.

There may be other underlying issues which need to be addressed. Start with your partner first by discussing these issues with him or her. Talking really helps. If they don't have the answers then perhaps it's time to seek professional help. Your doctor can help you with those arrangements.

I leave you with this, my friends. I know you'll find the strength within yourself if you take time and search and believe. Someone once said, "I would rather spend my life close to the birds than waste it wishing I had wings." I love that little saying. It makes you think and that's a good thing. Learn to enjoy each page you are turning in your book of life, and don't be afraid to write some new chapters. It's high time to stop always being in someone else's story and start being in your own. Mankind's most impenetrable secrets lie within our own head. No one can change his past. But his future . . . now that's a whole different story. Believing is just the beginning. It's that first baby step you have to take, but it is so worth taking.

I hope you are willing to consider some of my advice I've imparted to you within these pages. I really hate giving advice; it's so often useless. Hopefully, you won't find it so in this case.

I wish the very best to each of you and your families. May God bless you as He has me with much love, hope, strength, wisdom and courage.

Your friend, Carroll

RESOURCES

INTIMATE APPAREL FOR MEN AND WOMEN
and
Regular apparel for children/youth

Weir Comfees
P.O. Box 255
Alliston, ON
L9R 1Y8
Fax 705-434-1561
Email: admin@weircomfees.com
Website: www.weircomfees.com
They offer men's swim suits/unisex board shorts or surfer style swim-suits. They also produce a line of comfortable, safe, secure and afford-able undergarments, sleepwear, swimwear, pouch pockets, etc. in sizes for adult men, women/children/youth.

Ostomysecrets
877-613-6246
Email: info@ostomysecrets.com
Website: www.ostomysecrets.com
They offer apparel for women/men/children. Each staff member is not only a trained professional, but they each are ostomy patients them-selves. This certainly brings a lot of understanding and empathy to those of you who are interested in purchasing their product. It's com-forting to know that the salesperson you are working with actually has some idea of your illness.

My Coveralls
Email: csylvia@mycoveralls.com

Website: www.mycoveralls.com
335 Locust Knoll Dr.
Charles Town, West Virginia 25414
703-371-5964

They offer unique pouch covers for men/women/children

My Heart Ties
Email: info@myheartties.com
3910 Caughey Rd.   Suite 140
Erie, Pa. 16506
They offer beautifully feminine pouch covers for women

This list is just a small selection of the various types of lingerie, pouch covers, swimwear, underwear, etc. for men, women and children. I suggest you go to Google, Ask or Bing and type in ostomy lingerie or ostomy pouch covers, etc. You'll be able to find several websites that offer clothing for children/youth. You'll find all sorts of websites to explore. Have fun! I certainly did.

OSTOMY POUCH DEODORIZERS

Hollister- (M9), Triad Medical (Ostofresh), ReliaMed drops, Montreal Ostomy (Stop Plus Odor Eliminator), Smith & Nephew (Banish II liquid)

If you go to Google, Bing, or Ask, you'll discover several types of deodorants for ostomy pouches and you'll get a very diverse list. Do the same for problems with gas or ask your local pharmacist to assist you.

A new product and my new best friend. Poo-Pourri. It's for spritzing in the toilet *before* you eliminate your waste. They even make a purse or pocket size. And, yes, it reaslly works. It's not made for your pouch. Just for the toilet. When you leave the bathroom, your leave no unwanted traces that you've ever been there.

Acknowledgements

My hat is off to all who have helped in the writing of this book. All who have given unselfishly in their support. And, there were many. It would not have been possible without the unwavering encouragement, confidence, and love from *Team deCarle*.

My husband, Arthur, you have been my greatest cheerleader. My rock. Always listening, offering wise guidance, and much love. And when I needed a *literal* swift-kick, you never hesitated.

My children, Courtney, Mac, his wife Jennifer, and my grandchildren, Alexander, Cameron, Trey and Harry, you have been my inspiration. I'm deeply grateful for your devotion, support and understanding and for your giving of time, loving hearts and many memories. May your paths be traveled with ease and grace. With serenity, love, and much joy. As you reach beyond the stars in fulfillment of your dreams, may you do it with dignity, beneficence of spirit, forgiveness, humility, and the love of God always in your heart.

Thank you, Trey, for teaching Nana how to do puzzles again. I'll always remember your patience. A one and a half year old little boy and his Nana sitting together on the floor, you carefully showing me how to pick up each puzzle piece by the tiny knob, while attempting to place it where it belonged on the puzzle board. You didn't care that my stroke restricted me in having the dexterity and mental acuity to do a simple thing like a small child's puzzle. I was simply, your Nana. Never once were you annoyed with my inabilities. You had the patience of Job, my darling boy.

I owe an unimaginable debt of gratitude to George and Bobbie Decaire, for everything they did for me and my family in our time of need. There are no words sufficient enough to express how I feel. You are the definition of the word, *friends*. You are true gifts from God and I shall love, cherish, and keep you in a very special place in my heart, forever. And, George, I know you are looking down from above and smiling.

A special thanks to my dear friend Lisa Codianne Fowler. Your legendary trips across the street from your house to mine, in bathrobe and slippers, in the dead of night, when I was certain I'd lost everything on my computer and with a few clicks of my mouse you made it magically re-appear. Without your help, encouragement, and love, I cannot imagine where I'd be.

To my best friends for more than forty years, Barbara, Pete, and Bruce Farrow. You've always been there in good times and bad. I cherish you and thank you for your undying love, affection, unbelievable friendship and gift of family. You are a real treasure.

To my longtime, techno-savvy friend and fellow author, Harv Hollek, thanks for fifty years of memories and to Lizabeth for sharing you with me. I love you both. And as you smile down from above, my friend, I know you are proud.

I owe an immense debt of gratitude to everyone at the Methodist Hospital and Mayo Clinic, in Rochester, Minnesota, for all you did to ensure I returned home to the loving arms of my family and friends. And a special debt of gratitude to Dr. O. H. Beahrs. You were simply . . . my miracle worker. My many months spent at your hospital were made less frightening and far more compassionate by all your employees beginning with not only the talented team of doctors and nurses, but down to the maintenance people who cleaned my room daily.

After surgery, and finally able to eat real food, the young man who cleaned my windows weekly, offered to take his lunch hour and drive across town to buy me a chocolate chip cookie, simply because I'd mentioned I was craving one. And the real kicker is this. When he returned, cookies in hand and I asked how much I owed him for his efforts, his answer was merely . . . *not a thing. I wanted to do it because of all the months I'd spent cleaning your windows, you never once complained about anything. You always found the strength to smile and to ask about my day, my family, my schooling, and how I was doing. Never did you forget to thank me for cleaning your windows. You truly cared about me. I was happy to be able to do something special for you.* That young man refused any remuneration for his simple act of kindness.

This was the type of spirit that surrounded my life on a daily basis at Methodist Hospital; those willing to go above and beyond their normal duties to see to my needs, no matter what they were. You were truly an exceptional group of compassionate professionals. Every one of you.

To my dear friend Pattie Meades, for many long months of driving me back and forth to hospitals, rehab, and for having patience in making me feel comfortable in my very *uncomfortable* new skin.

Thank you to Dr. Thomas O'Malley, who was there when I needed you most.

To my editor, my friend, Susan Haley, I thank you for everything. I really could not have done it without your hard work and belief in my abilities as a writer. You showed me how to allow the baby bird to leave the nest to fly on her own. Thanks for believing in me. You are the jewel in my literary crown.

And, I want to especially thank you, the readers, who have graciously allowed me to share my journey with you. I hope I have given you an insightful glimpse into the life of an ostomy patient. A Crohn's patient. I thank you from the bottom of my heart and I look forward, with great privilege, to meeting with you either in person or on the Internet.

Carroll

Made in the USA
Columbia, SC
06 May 2018